GOING REAL

The Value of Design in the Era of PostCapitalism

Marco Petroni
Giovanni Innella

Foreword by
Craig Bremner

Afterword by
Angela Rui

Series in Design

VERNON PRESS

www.vernonpress.com

In the Americas:
Vernon Press
1000 N West Street,
Suite 1200, Wilmington,
Delaware 19801
United States

In the rest of the world:
Vernon Press
C/Sancti Espiritu 17,
Malaga, 29006
Spain

Series in Design

Library of Congress Control Number: 2019939876

ISBN: 978-1-62273-793-2

Also available: 978-1-62273-788-8 [Paperback, Premium Color];

978-1-62273-605-8 [Hardback, Premium Color]; 978-1-62273-740-6 [PDF, E-Book]

Cover designed by Vernon Press.
Cover image by Agata Jaworska and Giovanni Innella

Grateful acknowledgment is made to Editoriale Domus S.p.A. for the use of excerpts of some articles, to Planar Books for publishing the original version of this manuscript in Italian, and to all the authors who kindly provided the visuals in this book.

Table of contents

Foreword

By Craig Bremner

DESIGN IN ANY ERA: Going-For-Real

To begin to think about the accelerating transformation of the world by design, first, we have to see this change as a product of social transformation and not, as is mostly understood by the accelerationists, by transforming technology and capital to bring about this change at some future juncture. This has always been an uncomfortable position for design, which, by the mid-nineteenth century under the irresistible influence of the idea of utopia, had come to consider the social as a condition of design (not the other way around). But by now it should be clear that this historic design process has been ground down by flows of capital and people, and it is the flows of people urbanizing the planet that make transformation a social project not a technological project. I am certain it's not the aim of this book to illustrate a history of design, but that is what it does, and it's a very different type of history of design that comes from the authors' reliance on the proponents of the coming accelerated culture. By focusing on new 'projects' that stretch the possibilities of design to test new limits and boundaries, GOING REAL presents a new landscape for design in the coming topological culture. Rushing into a new topology of relations leaves behind it, not invisible but as traces, the several phases that have comprised the history of design[ing]. In this history, it is relatively easy to demonstrate these phases of design history because they are represented via projects that find their way into the first stories and the early exhibitions concerned with design as an emergent form of shaping the world. In short, one can state that the phases of design history were two: the TAXONOMIC phase and the CARTOGRAPHIC phase.

The TAXONOMIC phase concerned with the classification of design by category of design (e.g. industrial v. graphic), type of object/image/designer and some contextual details (e.g. country of origin). This mode of historicity was codified by the first exhibiting institutions (mainly museums) and exemplified in the influential design exhibition "Italy: The New Domestic Landscape" at MoMA in 1972. Following the taxonomic was the CARTOGRAPHIC phase concerned with locating design in space/time/market as exemplified in nationalist design styles – Danish/Italian/Japanese/etc. The cartographic phase was also codified by the exhibiting institutions (still in museums) and captures all the historic/current/future surveys of designers or design moments, which were all configured by the politics of branding manufacturing prowess and summarized by a marque to lure consumers "Made in COUNTRY".

The stories – and most of the histories – of design were told and/or exhibited in one form or another via these two modes of narration. For most of the relatively brief period in which design's history has been told (and re-told) design has only momentarily embraced the real. Victor Papanek's 'Design for the Real World' (1984) was far too real for design, because locked in with the infinite possibilities at the core of design's boundless opportunism, Papanek demanded infinite responsibility. Attempts to get closer to the real came about with the advent of innovation replacing the idea, and design's story was recalibrated into what I think of as the SYNTHETIC phase – the concern with new developments in methods, materials, practices and the advent of the design of nothing (otherwise known as services) that have the potential to affect people differently. This phase is exemplified in Paola Antonelli's numerous exhibitions at MoMA. In contrast to these more or less solid phases, we are now in a POST-CONTENT phase based on a system of global flows of potentially infinite linkages to information – the coming topological culture - that now require less of designers' creativity than the designer's almost non-existent editing skills.

GOING REAL is deeply immersed in what has and/or will follow the solid phases of both history and the technology that now defines our engagement with space and time. And this time is under acceleration as the book repeats – capitalism (design's patron) is postcapitalism, human (design's missing subject) is posthuman, the Anthropocene (only just coined but already contested) is post-Anthropocene, functionalist (design's problem-solving mantra) is post-functionalist, Fordist (the assembly line initiated not in Detroit but in Chicago slaughterhouses) is post-Fordist, industrial (the genetics of design) is post-industrial, and contemporaneity (itself only temporary) is post-contemporaneity. All of these 'posts', all of this 'after', all of this 'that which will follow', add up to the accelerated culture that the book documents in a series of incisive case studies.

Therefore, the logic applied to this book, while not explicitly building on these historic phases, assumes knowledge of where design has come from in order to investigate the relationships between design and the flows of information it must now edit in order to make sense of its position. To help find one's way the two common words Going and Real become a beguiling phrase as the title of this book – GOING REAL - and the amateur grammarian in me is a little surprised by their instant complexity. With the phrase GOING REAL what do the authors intend? And with a significant portion of the contents informed by the proponents of accelerationism GOING REAL urges design to pick up speed. But in order to address the 'post-' we need to revisit the 'pre-'

so that the 'after' that will become the 'future' as 'post-something' is recognizable by contrast to the long 'before'. But the grammar of the two words GOING and REAL is not simple. GOING can be an adjective, noun (gerund) and verb. And REAL can be both adverb and noun. If you explore the possibilities of its grammar you get the following prescient combinations;

> Going Real = adjective + adverb = an attribute that modifies a verb (in this case the future of a reality) – **The future…really**

> Going Real = adjective + noun = an attribute of a thing (in this case the reality of a future) – **The really future**

> Going Real = noun + adverb = the thing of a modifier (in this case the future of reality) – **The future reality**

> Going Real = noun + noun = the thing of a thing (in this case the future of the future and/or the reality of reality) – **The future future and/or the real real**

> Going Real = verb + adverb = acting on a modifier (in this case the future real) – **The future real**

> Going Real = verb + noun = acting on a thing (in this case the real future) – **The real future**

Regardless of the combination GOING REAL makes sense of its entangled syntax and by exploring its rules its argument – The Value of Design in the Era of Postcapitalism – simply gets stronger. I will explain.

The Future… Really

Any and every discussion of design involves some notion of a future that in some way will be influenced by design or hold some sort of future for design. And as I said, at the outset of this discussion always winds up in the genre of utopia – it is unavoidable for the simple fact that design's predilection for what-might-become is utopian. Ironically, this weakness for possible future scenarios is, post-everything, now better expressed as what-might-not-become, and GOING REAL uses this recent inevitability as its springboard. In this manner it shares many of the qualities of the illustrative utopia; it is a book where a challenging new idea of design has been fused with the concept of a becoming ideal depiction of design illustrated by case studies aimed to give us the possibility of future plans; and the future is in desperate need of plans. But long before the illustrative utopia emerged more or less a century ago, the narrative utopia had been circulating in increasingly incalculable numbers for about 400 years. In this – its original form – it was clear that the planned conditions aimed at conditioning society made life itself conditional, producing purposefully uncomfortable *planned futures*. But very recently (in a geological time being called the Anthropocene or Capitalocene or, in this book, post-Anthropocene) the planet has taken over the planning of our future.

That future plans always became planned futures only came to light in the early 20th Century and the limiting prospects of these futures are enacted daily as the idea of design was replaced by the image – first the image of the urban city and then the image of the planetary city and now the dream images of an interplanetary city funded by tech-billionaires. All these images/dreams were illustrated by the radical designers as a technological exit from utopia but now they have been reprised as literal means of re-entering the non-place of utopia on the one island we share. With this background, for design to be going anywhere, the Real must confront the conflict between the Idea of design versus some Ideal of design[ing]. However, because of its media definition, the very idea of design invites pursuit of the ideal. And educational enhancement has laid the path to the ideal designer. Enhancement was developed around the regime of organization and has become classically scientific. The regime is now so successful that it is imitated everywhere. Therefore, the idea of the design produced the imitation of both the regime and the designer. The imitation is now the Ideal and the media transmit this creation. Design no longer needs an idea, giving rise to a question vexing all dimensions of design – if the ideal (now a derivative) no longer needs an idea (an original), can design (endless imitation) produce an idea of design? An answer requires knowing what to look for. And perhaps we shouldn't look at the means of enhancement (talent identification and education), or enhancing the means (via increasingly accelerated technologies), which both pursue the ideal. If we look from outside the regime, then the ideal designer is playing to a skeptical public with little trust in the idea of design. So, without an idea, the ideal of design is now a fragile media invention with no moral reference. But now the idea of the discipline of design doesn't seem to exist, and its ideal exists on another playing field defined by the media. The net result is the ideal has no feel for the idea, and the idea has no effect on the ideal. If we accept this scenario, we have to ask whether we still participate in the idea of design? The answer from GOING REAL is an unqualified yes.

The Really Future

What happens when we go about navigating the utopian idea as the realization of an ideal or a contract (i.e. how to achieve that ideal)? The narrative utopia has always been understood to function not as a possible future scenario, but as a critique of existing conditions and is studied in literature under the genre of satire. By contrast, the function of the much later illustrative utopia has become highly problematic. In the late nineteenth century, there was a seismic shift in the concept of utopia when the depiction of idealized space was grafted onto the urban planning imaginary rapidly seducing us into attempting to construct idealized spaces. The same happened not long after, under the guidance of the Bauhaus with its idealized types of objects, and now again under the illusion of techno-populism idealized services. Services that make us believe we belong. By imaging society as a product of ideal space the 'illustrated plan' highlighted economic, social and political problems which planning then solved leading to the design of planned futures. Early in the twentieth century new cities and new suburbs on the outskirts of old cities appeared to validate this idealized form of plan. Detroit (featured in this book) is a typical example where the existence of the idealized object – the car – created the conditions for the ideal suburban life. As a result, what was once a conditional critique became a conditioning device. From that moment the idea of the future became unnatural. Not quite artificial, but no longer natural in the way that the future had always been perceived to be real. However, as David Harvey explains, the future has already been mortgaged; he writes "One of the things about debt is that it tends to foreclose the future—you have already spent the future," Harvey says. "It is very difficult to have an imagination of something radically different when your future is already pinned to some continuation of capital" (cited in Carlson S., 2014).

The Future Reality

One of the exits from the moral weight of the history of progress has been the fashion for disruption, which Jill Lepore (2018) explains "…emerges in the 1990s as progress without any obligation to notions of goodness. And so *disruptive innovation*, which became the buzzword of change in every realm in the first years of the 21st century, including higher education, is basically destroying things because we can and because there can be money made doing so" (cited in Goldstein E., 2018).

The Future Future and/or The Real Real

When Giorgio Agamben wrote "utopia is the very topicality of things" (cited in Salzani C, 2012), he meant belonging to a particular place, but that is increasingly difficult to register in the collective imaginary in the coming topological culture that is skimming across the networked surface of everyday life. In order to imagine designing for a future that is an increasing accumulation of networked images of no-place in particular, we resort to making willful mis-representations of life. Sentimentality is defined as the misrepresentation of the past to suit our future purposes, so both the real and the future are primarily sentimental (Midgley M., 1979). Restoring the deteriorating images of the actions we still seem to like to call design is a sentimental project that only enables us to live in the permanent present – the topical now. In this vein, the future will remain irreparable because the imaginary images necessary for that future will always be in need of constant repair. Fortunately, GOING RE-AL makes the case that it is a toolbox in which we can find useful tools to repair and reset the modern project.

The Future Real

The launch of the modern project was the realization that we could imagine change and that change could take place animated by design. That we can imagine change animates both the future possible and the future real. Design's predilection for opportunism turns every 'as-if' into an imperative 'should-be' driven by Capital turning the future into a money-making deal that is the contractual utopia of every design opportunism.

The Real Future

In stark contrast to the design imagination, for the few that own the planet, the planet has become a destination increasingly like a festival (as satirized by Ettore Sottsass) in which we are allowed to engage in their society of the spectacle (as denigrated by Guy Debord) transforming the brief periods we are not working into utopian tourism where we search for islands where we can pretend to be native/natural for two weeks (Augé M., 2005). From its invention, the site of utopia has almost always been depicted as an island. What isn't explained about the attraction of the island for the setting of utopia is this: utopia has never been about an ideal location – its concern is the location of ideas. The island has always served as the platform for isolating future of ideas from their contemporary failure. And despite the neutralizing apocalyptic scenarios we confront we still need to locate ideas for a future of being together on the one island we share. But on this island we share, there are a few conceptual islands that have formed that help locate how we might think about any possible future – and this is what GOING REAL does well – its case-studies are islands of possibilities in oceans of debt and doubt. When the planet turned from rural to urban the rural had always been an idealized setting for the narrative utopia preferably getting away from the hell that is our neighbors. But when the illustrative utopia emerged, it found the city too beguiling to ignore and soon flying cars filled the space between heroic towers. However, these fantastically illustrated cities are in fact rural islands, Arcadian locations cloistered by agricultural landscapes. As the city became a fantasy everywhere that was not-city, the regional was set on a collision course with new kinds of limits: limits to biodiversity, and limits to the flows of energy and water. From this emerged a contrasting scenario of increasingly unlimited digital flows. Such flows were mostly methods of genetic experimentation and forms of entertainment. The result was that rural islands were left to compete globally for population and productivity. The deterioration of this landscape has resulted in more flows of populations into cities whose opportunities are inversely proportional to the flow producing what Mike Davis called a Planet of Slums (Davis M., 2006).

In contrast to the rural, all of the accelerating flows of data on individuals, populations, ecologies, economics, cities and other subjects are creating informatic islands of rich media producing exhaustive visual evidence that contrasts 'as-is' (or as-it-is) with 'as-if' (or as-it-might or should-be). How we navigate the informatic island is a mix of a techno-populism that has delivered no more than the infinite accumulation of unnecessary stuff in exchange for invasive forms of data analytics and this later is highly profitable. The expanding 'islands' of virtual life include the vast gaming world that is either utopian in nature or called something like 'Utopia Version…' have become network islands. The ability to interact with the informatics island via the contemporary form of utopia known as participatory culture and its networked contexts such as social media, open source culture, and 'prosumer' tendencies contract us all into the project of hyper-financed (post-capitalist?) techno-utopianism.

The network islands are therefore booming nostalgic or sentimental misrepresentations playing out in our preference for the preservation of 'as-is', or, the plummeting projections of 'what-might-not-become' – compared to 'as-is' – causing us to resort to our memories so we can recognize change. This nostalgia – this longing to return home – is a romance with myriad personal fantasies and any project about the future always has a nostalgia component that has been seen before, and always returns design to its home (Boym S., 2007). From the first turning of the industrial revolution, design emerges as a way to communicate with the machine, but the machine rapidly made the design idea into an image of itself, and this is a critical moment absent from the history of design. The machine made the idea into an image of itself; first, as an imitation of the machine; and second, as an imitation of the imaginary capacity of design. Almost instantly the idea became an infinite imitation of itself, but we can no longer perceive this, and worse, still we accept this as natural. But the imitation of imitation has resulted in derivation and the derivative is a precarious financial product that functions by insuring against change. Change is now simply a way to make money. Without the capacity to imagine change and with the future foreclosed, the prospects for the future of the island we call Earth remaining our ideal location are plummeting.

As I have said utopia is not about the ideal location: it is about the location of ideas. The danger for the project of being together on a populous planet in unprecedented proximity is that the conditions are entirely dependent on the capacity to imagine change for which we need to locate ideas. Under these conditions it is possible to think of a future reality as science fiction has done for decades and as Timothy Morton does when describing the Anthropocene, "an undead place of zombies, viroids, junk DNA, ghosts, silicates, cyanide, radiation, demonic forces, and pollution…. When the charm of world is dispelled, we find ourselves in the emergency room of ecological coexistence" (Morton T., 2013). It is also possible to think of the future as already delimited, as did a raft of scientists, who in 2009 published in the journal Nature a new study on the planet's carrying capacity entitled "A safe operating space for humanity" (Rockström, J. et al., 2009). The same data that enabled the imaginativeness of a 'safe' operating space was in fact initially enabled by "the integration of […] data sets into a comprehensive portrait of global climate by the long-term military investment in supercomputing"; an investment prompted by the need to trace the effects of nuclear tests (Masco J., 2010). The same tests prompted the development of the scientific scenario called the Nuclear Winter, whose bleak prospect then became the subject of countless horror films full of radiated zombies. Benjamin Bratton thinks otherwise. He predicts that "…the best of all possible news is that, should we survive the Anthropocene, it will not be as humans." (Bratton B., 2013).

In this bleak context what does GOING REAL signify for design? One way to answer this question is to ask several more such as the authors of the World Happiness Report who ask, "What will guide humanity in the Anthropocene: advertising, sustainability, community, or something else? What is the path to happiness?" (Helliwell J. et al., 2012). A possible way to answer what is becoming an endless string of questions about the design of change in a climate of unknowable transformations comes from Peter Sloterdijk who says "The most important fact of Modernity is not that earth orbits the sun, but that money orbits earth" (cited in van Tuinen S., 2009). Another possible answer comes from the authors of GOING REAL who write about a geologically post-Anthropocene planet whose post-contemporaneity is accelerating it into a post-industrial/post-Fordist/post-functionalist/post-capitalist/post-human cosmos. Their book, GOING REAL, could serve as a post-operative manual for the recuperation of spaceship earth.

Introduction

"The value of what he was doing was immeasurable.
Wasn't it always like this?"

Il Brevetto del Geco
by Tiziano Scarpa (2016)

This book is an attempt to investigate the core of the contradictions emerging from the world of contemporary design. New economic relations, the technological influence and algorithms of working processes, the margins of creativity and autonomy that seem to be profiled in a scenario of profound transformation are the themes chosen to define a multiplicity of issues that denote a return to reality in the design of our times. What is the value of design in the world we live in? How do we engage with this world? These are some of the questions that determine the choice and the analysis of a perspective whose objective is to restore the centrality of critical thinking and to redefine its role in a more general cultural sense. The friction exercised by an increasingly violent and pervasive capitalism clashes with the subjective aptitude to build relationships, to share and cooperate in a more inclusive way. In the design world, there is an increasing need for new resistance and responses, for new attention on the manual skills of the processes, for the sustainability of materials, the precariousness of the solutions, and for the imagination of new and flexibility forms of design and of designing. The urgency to generate trajectories, even if as-yet indeterminate, capable of affecting our daily life, of populating new territories of theoretical and operational investigation, gains again a central role. Contemporary design must accept the responsibility of proposing itself as a device for shaping a vision and an interpretation of reality, pushing itself to prefigure a possible future. It is with such spirit that we welcome the readers to what we think being extremely interesting and challenging times.

And this is also how Slavoj Zizek defines our contemporaneity, a new condition in which the economic crisis has become permanent and is now our way of life (Zizek S., 2010). A radical change that has shattered certainties and opportunities, producing a sense of widespread loss and the shadow of uselessness for entire generations. Since every form of design is transformation, and therefore production of new worlds, we need to focus on an assessment that is not only economic, but also social, emotional, and political. The task of the true designer of today is not to dissipate the mysteries of our societies, but to always reveal new ones. Design must measure itself according to an unprecedented condition, determined by needs and scenarios that are under construction, generated by financial capitalism, by social media, by the spread of artificial intelligence, by Big Data. It is a world characterized by human relations that are increasingly determined by analyses and predictive behaviors aiming to anticipate the formation of defined subjectivity and to eliminate the possibility of conflicts and reactions. All of the services of a global giant such as Amazon are based on this logic of anticipation, of the estimated determination of anyone's desires. And who can tell us that even future governments are not configured in a similar way? This book is conceived as an open process, a sort of toolbox in which you can find useful tools to generate a dialogue that goes beyond specific disciplinary areas, and that tries to explore the new operational and conceptual areas we engage with in our work and social lives. It may seem that this book sometimes takes extreme and speculative tangents, but if it does, it is only to better understand the world in which we live.

If you have studied product design or industrial design, you will have come across the "factor 4" dogma. This is a sort of magical formula stating that, if you make a spreadsheet and input all the costs of producing an object, and then multiply them by 4, you should get something close to the selling price of the product in question. Well, if you've ever worked as a designer, you'll have realized that this rule is a big lie. It is no longer applicable to the industry in which we are working. The designer is that professional who reflects on how to manipulate materials (including time and people's skills) to create added value. However, this improvement factor of design is difficult to measure. There are designers who are able to take materials and economic processes at low cost or of no value and produce things that have very high prices on the market. On the other hand, there are designers who start with very precious materials and are able to generate processes so that the final product is free. Often, these designers are not even designers, per se. They are community leaders, entrepreneurs or simple individuals without specific skills, but with a vision and an attitude to stimulate and engage with others.

The world we live in rebounds between these extremes: from the extremely expensive and exclusive design for the few, to the free design for all; from the design of tangible things to that of social innovations. The value of design is no longer measurable in the final price and not even in corporate turnovers. Precisely for this reason, we have started out on an exploratory journey to understand who, where, and how it creates value, and what kind of value is actually generated. From the social, to the political and economic value, we must start to reflect on all types of design that the design world has overlooked. We must keep in mind that the work of the designer is made of mobility, relationality, affectivity, the ability to cross over among different disci-

plinary areas, adherence to the temporality of the project, alternation between independence and corporate bonds, total merging of work and of life,
coexistence between entrepreneurship and creativity, creation and management of increasingly complex issues.

What is the measure of all of this? The three chapters that make up this book
try to suggest possible answers. The first chapter proposes a theoretical framework aimed at redefining the value of design in connection with the rethinking
of a social environment that is scourged by the failures of neoliberal capitalism.
Detroit is the point of reference here. Detroit has been chosen as a field of investigation to identify a crucial step in the transformation of the operational possibilities offered by a *zero-degree* design that demonstrates a clear change in the
factors involved. It is a matter of identifying a precarious social condition in
which work and life overlap, and awareness becomes a process of subjectivation, of emancipation outside the prevailing logic. "New work, new culture" is
the cultural movement created in Detroit, a city that is experiencing an epochal
change. The idea of work that we have today has existed only for the past two
hundred years, forcing individuals to do what they 'must' do, not what they
'want' to do. Detroit represents an exceptional opportunity to promote a new
culture of work that puts the relationship among people at the center. We must
imagine working for a community and in so doing, creating community (Bergmann F., 2014). The practices of the transdisciplinary collective Akoaki who is
redesigning Detroit's cultural and economic landscape are moving precisely in
this direction. A vision of the project emerges as a connective tissue capable of
creating collaborative platforms, ecosystems based on the sharing of information, knowledge, techniques in which power is not held in the hands of a few.
In Akoaki's vision design becomes the tool to bring wealth and economic sustainability to those who participate in and benefit from it. It is about actively
looking at the possibilities offered by the failures of capitalism, in order to open
up scenarios in perpetual mutation that continually produce new ideas and that
often, when encountered for the first time, seem like something alien, like abstract concepts. It is precisely in the folds of rampant passivity that design re-
gains its evolutionary and improving attitude, becoming a powerful tool for
transmitting knowledge. The necessary factor for this to find a link to the reality
of our everyday lives, is the formation of a critical gaze capable of framing a
context made up of real people emerging from a series of specific urban and
cultural circumstances.

The second chapter finds references in the concepts expressed by the British
economist Paul Mason in his essay, *PostCapitalism: A Guide to our Future*, in
which he defines a scenario marked by a subtle and profound transformation of
the logic of Capital under the pressure of technological innovation (Mason P.,
2015). The diffusion of digital culture has radically changed the organization of

work, generating a paradigm shift that apparently presents itself as more inclusive and horizontal than the vertical-hierarchical plan that has always distinguished the Fordist/Taylorist organization of work, based on the rigidly predefined sequence: design, production, marketing. In reality, current capitalism, marked by the relational dematerialization of its constituent elements, lives and proliferates in a paradoxical contradiction. On the one hand, there is a growing importance of cognitive/creative/intellectual work as a lever for the production of wealth and, on the other hand, we witness its devaluation in both salary and professional terms. This is a condition that is based precisely on heterogeneity, on the fragmentary identity of the subjects involved who are pulled into the network of competition for the assessment of their productions. This profound singularization and operational solitude, sugar-coated and suppressed by social networks, do not allow the formation of focus groups, but rather refer to a multitude of differentiated singularities, each with their own professional perceptions. In this scenario, precariousness becomes a structural, existential and generalized condition without any safety net. This is the result of the financialization process that marked the advent of a capitalism favoring the exploitation of network and learning economies. If we look at Mason's thoughts, we notice that this neoliberal system has come to an end and must necessarily be replaced by a network economy based on knowledge and sharing. As Mason observes, technology has introduced ways of working and consuming that challenge the economic system based on the law of supply and demand. Free-time, network activities and gratuitousness will be the currency of the future (Mason P., 2016). In defining and structuring this new economic context, design acquires a role of primary importance. It surpasses and exceeds a field that wants it limited to the world of material objects, to open up to the definition and critical interrogation of online identity, to interactivity with personal devices, to the search for new materials, interfaces, networks, systems, infrastructures, data, organisms, and genetic codes. The opportunity for redefining the social and cultural role of the designer comes into play, which, as a subject of the system of capitalist exploitation, goes back to questioning what is most urgent in cognitive terms, or in cultural terms in the widest sense. It is precisely reality, our immanent day-to-day, the terrain on which designers must and should confront themselves with the awareness that the value of the production depends not only on the value of one's own production but also on one's own destiny. These are the most complex and unavoidable issues of our time, those with which we absolutely must deal. Calais and the evacuated temporary city of the Jungle are the epicenter of the thorny issue of migrants, a population of 65 million people living in a suspended condition, without predefined rights and identities. The second chapter reviews some projects that were created without media hype, in the daily existential precariousness of these people in movement, confirming that "architecture and design are the litmus tests of our identity as human beings", as stated by Sean Anderson, curator of *Insecurities: Tracing Displacement and Shelter*, a recent exhibition at MoMA in New York (Anderson S., 2016).

The third chapter tries to investigate possible biopolitics of value by putting the human body at the center of its field of action, with all its aporias. Design observes and engages with political theory, economics, philosophy, ethics, and with science and biotechnology. The human body is seen as a battlefield of different and often conflicting forces. Universal themes such as birth, sex, safety, and health become useful elements to explore, with a microscopic gaze, the role of design in the development of scientific research, but, above all, regarding ethical and behavioral issues. This is a speculative attitude associated with the field of critical design – patronized by the likes of Fiona Raby and Anthony Dunne –, but that needs to be to put into action as a design methodology helping and fostering transdisciplinary interactions. A vision of design that links and challenges the theoretical implications of the recent debate on the Anthropocene: in a world transformed by humans, we are pushed to consider hybrid hypotheses that result from the combination of what is natural and what is artificial, to the point of reconsidering the very essence of the human body in a transhumanist or post-human sense. In an environment that is irremediably marked by disasters of ecology, energy, and overpopulation, the experiments that design and science elaborate in the laboratory will, sooner or later, end up being shared by ever larger groups of users. The challenge is to find balances able to create a better era than this one, devoted as it is to environmental destruction and the exploitation of biotechnological innovation in the name of profit. This is the new task that many designers of our time intend to carve out in a world marked by technological acceleration, in which knowledge and the power of transformations have never been so great. We need to work with new ways to define an environment in which the designer is the creator, engineer, and permanent stimulator of a new and sustainable humanism. In search of harmony with new ways of living, governing and determining ourselves, the human body becomes the new speculative referent for designers. The design of the individual and of the community – no longer of the mere objects – suggests strategies of subjectivation and the freeing-up of new spaces of action for designers. This final chapter, therefore, closes a path that starts with *place*, continues with *community*, and ends with the *individual*, one's body and the need to determine and govern oneself.

As mentioned, the book collects a series of reflections on economics, ethics and societal matters. In doing so, Going Real adds a series of real or speculative design references, becoming an opportunity to historicize topics widely discussed elsewhere, but that design critique – unlike designers – has not yet fully assimilated. Even more simply, this book proposes itself as an enactment of concepts such as Accelerationism, Postcapitalism, Post-Anthropocene, transhumanism, illustrated with the referencing materials provided by contemporary design in a broad sense.

Chapter 1

Going There

"The great moments are those in which one world dies and another takes its place."

Freedom
by Jonathan Franzen (2010)

Towards a definition of value

On Thursday, July 18, 2013, Michigan Governor Rick Snyder uploaded a video on YouTube in which he declared that "Detroit has gone bankrupt with debts" (Snyder R., 2013). After decades of corruption, sky-high crime, economic decline, and depopulation, Motor City, the capital of the US automotive industry, follows in the footsteps of General Motors and Chrysler in 2009, in a bankruptcy that has no precedent in recent economic history. With 1.85 million inhabitants and over 200 thousand workers, in 1950, Detroit was the fourth largest American metropolis, before experiencing an ineluctable decline. The exodus of the white population towards the wealthier suburbs, which increased after the civil rights protests at the end of the 60s, further impoverished the city. This movement of people reduced taxable income, triggering a vicious circle. The municipality had less and less money to pay for public services, which made the city ever less welcoming, and further encouraged exodus. As stated by a study of the American Institute of Architects, large parts of the middle class moving to the suburbs resulted in the closure and abandonment of offices and shops in the center. The remaining population is poorer and more dependent on public services (Lomas R., 1999).

The automobile crisis, with the loss of thousands of jobs, took care of the rest; images of ruined buildings, of entire abandoned blocks, and other content for *ruin porn* – the art of immortalizing ruined buildings loved by tourists and detested by the inhabitants – have become some of the most typical emblems of the American industrial crisis. It is in one of these abandoned buildings that American director Jim Jarmusch decides to set one of his most dramatically political films, Only Lovers Left Alive, presented at the Cannes Film Festival of 2013. It is a twisted tale in which the last romantics left in our world are vampires. In such a world, human beings are zombies; they have lost interest in life, in knowledge, and are heading towards a sad apocalypse. In contrast, Jarmusch's characters, Adam (Tom Hiddleston) and Eve (Tilda Swinton) are decadent and refined creatures, cultured and educated. Adam lives in a deserted, impoverished Detroit, devoting himself to the creation of marvelous electrical devices inspired by the ingenuity of Nikola Tesla.

A solitary inventor oppressed by a depression caused by the awareness of the decadence of the surrounding world. Everything around him seems on the verge of decay, from the house he lives in to the most essential relationships. The movie is a profound portrait and an acute metaphor for a world that has voraciously consumed its resources, whose inhabitants, unconscious zombies, contribute, through their abuses and excesses, to their own self-destruction. In this context, the protagonists of the film do not represent a danger to humanity; rather, they assume the role of astonished observers.

"Did you get my message?" Eve asks Adam, who responds: "I think so. I had a dream." This premise, oscillating between news/reality and fiction/cinema, locates us in a dimension of threatening suspension, a sort of *tabula rasa* in which we need to reset the instruments of reading and action in order not to lose our sense of orientation in the contemporary world. Detroit can be considered the archetype of a condition of our time, in which we can look at design to define where we are and where we might want to go. Without any guarantee, of course. Starting from the need to indicate new trajectories and operational opportunities, the interesting reflections of Nick Srnicek and Alex Williams are included in the essay *Inventing the Future: Postcapitalism and a World Without Work* (Srnicek N. and Williams A., 2016). Rather than a confused and defensive vision of a high-tech world that should be criminalized, this essay, instead, proposes a society that stimulates and identifies the possibility of emancipation oriented towards our future. The goal of the essay is to design a postcapitalist economy that is able to focus on the social value of material and immaterial production, thus freeing humanity from work, as well as developing technologies capable of expanding our freedom and autonomy. Any post-capitalist project necessarily requires the creation of new cognitive maps, political narratives, technological interfaces, economic models and mechanisms of collective control useful for organizing complex phenomena for the improvement of humanity (Srnicek N. and Williams A., 2016). It is an invitation not to resign ourselves to a single world model that is dominated by neoliberal logic, but instead, to revive an imaginative commitment to the future. In this imaginative effort of production, design is called upon to grasp the growing sophistication of technology to define a condition of everyday life in which people are no longer obliged to be workers; in which production and distribution are democratically delegated to a largely automated infrastructure.

For the authors of the essay, it is necessary to combine a utopian fantasy with patient, organizational work, both of which are needed to wrest the future from the clutches of the dominant logic. We all know that today 'modernization' often translates into job cuts, and the privatization of basic rights such as health and all public services. The logic behind this idea of modernity is based on the famous slogan coined by Margaret Thatcher: "there is no alternative", a claim that legitimizes an economic-political vision that highlights an apparent lack of alternatives to the neoliberal system. The free market, capitalism, and globalization seem the only viable path for the development of a modern society. This vision has come to an end. The idea of competitive subjects devoted to continuous self-improvement in every aspect of life; enforced, continuous training to meet employment requirements; and the constant need for self-reinvention are all elements of the neoliberal collage. Under these conditions, it is no surprise that anxiety is proliferating in contemporary societies. Stress, depression, and attention deficit disorders are increasingly common psychological responses in the world around us. Neoliberalism has thus become the form of our existence, our way of relating to others. In other words, it is not only politicians, entrepreneurs, media elites, and academics who have signed up with this world view, but also workers, students, migrants, and everyone else. Neoliberalism creates this subjectivity. A system that also produces within itself forms of organization that are not a second choice, but that are the shoots of a new system that we do not yet know and that deserves to be investigated (Berardi F., 2009).

We need to imagine a territory as a laboratory and incubator/catalyst of a new cultural perspective, capable of combining knowledge and subjects that interact on a global level with similar realities. An opportunity for the construction/experimentation of a sustainable system that, through design, brings into play skills, attitudes, and productions. True value is derived from an ecosystem designed as a sustainable enterprise based on the creation of a new sense of community. The need for new strategies in training and production is at the center of this community idea. The soul of this vision comprises communities of people who belong to the world of architecture, design, visual arts, new media, writing, music, performing arts, theatre, cinema. Those who work in close contact with the denizens of the places they inhabit. The aim is to generate new dynamics in the context of culture and production, to strengthen the visibility and recognition of the creative disciplines and their high educational value, creating opportunities and implementing relationships with analogous realities.

There is concrete evidence of these dynamics in the various urban agriculture initiatives implemented by the Michigan Urban Farming Initiative (MUFI). In the years following the failure of local governance, MUFI has provided Detroit residents with tools and opportunities to reclaim the urban spaces that have been abandoned, as a result of both commercial and social policies.

Thus, disused factories and private and public houses have become agricultural gardens, but, more important, they have become places of aggregation and production for new communities. These initiatives of social planning come from the grassroots level, and have then inspired urbanists at various levels to rethink the city as a succession of villages that share vacant lots, renamed as "opportunity areas" (Renn M.A., 2009). These projects are defined as an evolutionary path that poses an idea of work that is not synonymous with the precarious relationship between the designer and the client, but that instead is a capillary network capable of enhancing a widespread and collective creativity – or simply the desire for this.

The deep penetration of digital technologies into our lives – and in particular in the community of Detroit – has important consequences on the way we feel and experience objects (whether digital or analogue). This must also be taken into consideration when we think of a return to what is basic and necessary, including the production of food. Such a design approach takes a chance on the tangible and intangible values that define the identity of a territory, on its ability to systematize its endogenous resources, on its ability to manage and enhance the relationships among individuals and communities. We will focus on these aspects in the next paragraph, using Akoaki's work as a probe to better understand the role of technology in changing the dynamics of a city to be redefined socially and economically, but perhaps not culturally. The validity of this path has been shown by some recent acknowledgments, such as that of Unesco in 2015. Detroit, City of Design, is a clear identification and legitimization of an excitement that comes from the bottom up, that sees design as an inclusive and vital factor for the rebirth of the city. In an article published in the Wall Street Journal, Amy Chozick said:

> *"From Motown Records to Elmore Leonard, the city is rich in cultural legacy. No one expects a return to the glory days when Detroit was a symbol of entrepreneurialism and the automobile business helped make the U.S. the world's greatest economic power. But proponents say any jump-start can lift depressed spirits as well as spur lasting economic improvement"*
>
> *(Chozick A., 2010)*

1.1. Akoaki, "The Mothership", Detroit, Michigan, 2014.

Traditions, translations, betrayals are the key words to understanding how culture, the transmission of knowledge (*tradere* is the Latin root that links the three concepts) can be a living resource through which to imagine, to invent the present. Before pointing out some practices that are being developed in Detroit, we want to emphasize that now it is essential to review the theoretical and critical tools, in order to read the design scenarios of our time. Strategies and visions that seem to coagulate and come to life in Bruno Latour's research are also explicit in the exhibition *Reset Modernity!* at the ZKM in Karlsruhe (Latour B. and Leclerq C., 2016). A project developed in collaboration with Martin Guinard-Terrin, Christophe Leclercq, and Donato Ricci.

An ensemble of media and channels of communication triggers a reflection and indicate variations on how to approach our time, which is threatened by profound changes that are transforming the very essence of the environment in which we live. An attempt to explore and unveil what often does not immediately appear as visible in the world of things and images among which we live. *Reset Modernity!* is an exhibition project conceived as a device to manifest an invisible complexity. It is a transdisciplinary strategy of rethinking the concept of modernity that Latour began to confront in his 1991 cult essay *Nous n'avons jamais été modernes: Essais d'anthropologie symètrique* (Latour B., 1991). A reflection with an almost prophetic taste, in which the French philosopher delineates the inadequacy of many categories of thought, such as modernity and post-modernity, opening our eyes onto a hybrid and strongly interconnected reality. Nature and culture intertwine, forming a universe of stratified objects that require a collaborative gaze, in dialogue with knowledge, in order to capture more inclusive aspects that lead to a non-hierarchical, potentially more horizontal world. It is precisely this multiplicious and open sensitivity that animates the interesting German exhibition experiment. A path punctuated not by sections or thematic areas, but by six *Procedures* indicated as ways of resetting our sense of orientation in the global world.

> *"at a time of profound ecological mutation, such a compass is running in wild circles without offering much orientation anymore. This is why it is time for a reset. Let's pause for a while, follow a procedure and search for different sensors that could allow us to recalibrate our detectors, our instruments, to feel anew where we are and where we might wish to go. No guarantee, of course: this is an experiment, a thought experiment, a Gedankenausstellung"*

> *(Latour B. and Leclerq C., 2016)*

Procedure A, called *Relocalizing the Global*, is a rethinking of the notion of global that has, as its first point of reflection, the 1977 video made by Ray and Charles Eames for IBM: "Powers of Ten: a film dealing with the relative size of things in the universe and the effect of adding another zero." In it, a picnic on the shores of Lake Michigan near Detroit was transformed into a journey, from the most hidden meanderings of the cosmos to the very structure of the molecules that make it up. An investigation that we could consider typical of the modernist attitude well summarized in Ernesto Nathan Rogers's slogan, "from the spoon to the city" (1952).

This faith in being able to control every possible human declension has been in crisis for some time already. The curators propose a reset through the work of Andrès Jaque and the Office for Political Innovation, which re-enacts the Eames film, dividing it into several acts and scenes. In the new version, the authors concentrate their attention on economic, political, and social events that do not appear in the original film, underlining the shadowy areas of History and the absence of social criticism in the work. For Jaque, the Office is a space for exploring domains that tend to be hidden to designers and architects and remain reserved to experts, such as the purification of water and air through plants, the production of energy, and so on. The goal of such an approach to design is to disrupt the way societies are organized and find new opportunities for change. A programmatic necessity deepened also by the work of Peter Gallison and Robb Moss *Wall of Science* (2015) that relates to the Eames' video. This work questions faith in science by introducing into a scientific laboratory some stumbling blocks of unpredictability, which produce an expansion of knowledge and results. Another procedure, *From Lands to Disputed Territories*, takes as an archetype the investigation of the Arctic ice slab, a seemingly desolate land that could in the future generate widespread interest in the exploitation of resources.

Similarly, the work of the Italian collective Studio Folder, *Italian Limes* (2014), becomes extremely interesting for our analysis. *Italian Limes* is a multimedia installation that interrogates the borders between two places, especially if this border falls in an Alpine area that, due to the global warming of the planet, is melting rapidly, putting the whole ecosystem at risk. The Alpine watershed therefore becomes a mobile border that escapes the cartographic certainties – and consequently also the political ones – by changing the very concept of limit, of border. In their project, a set of strategically placed sensors, monitors the watershed – and therefore, border – between Austrian and Italy. The information is sent to a robotized pen that at given intervals of times, traces the line of the border on a map.

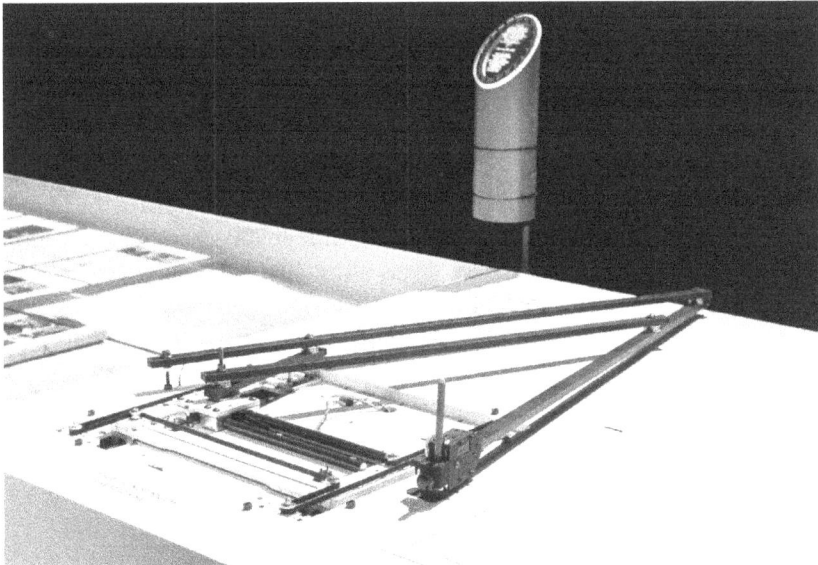

1.2. Studio Folder, "Italian Limes", Venice, Italy, 2014.

The final *Procedure* of *Reset Modernity!,* titled *Innovation not Hype*, reflects upon the theme of transformation. And it is the heroic *Toaster Project* (2009) by English designer Thomas Thwaites that concludes the exploration of this area, an indeterminate but necessary area of reflection regarding our time, from different and transdisciplinary perspectives. This final project by Thomas Thwaites opens many questions toward a rethinking of the concept of value. This is an adventurous project, developed during a nine-month trip from the home appliance store in the author's English town, through the mines of the United Kingdom, to his mother's yard, where, by modifying his parents' microwave oven, Twaites created a small foundry. Along the way, the designer acquires a series of information: he discovers that a common toaster consists of 404 separate parts, that the best way to melt metal in the home is to use a method found in a fifteenth-century treatise, and that plastic is almost impossible to produce from scratch. The result of this quixotic adventure is a disturbing, hand-made toaster that costs 250 times more than a common one, sold at market prices. Thwaites's project, told in a self-mocking diary-like book chronicling about the two thousand miles spent in remote places in the United Kingdom, allows us to reflect on the costs and dangers of our consumer culture, and in doing so, it reveals a lot about the organization of the contemporary world. Thomas Thwaites's project is to be entertained with as much as it is to be admired, for its courage to achieve something that is absolutely superfluous like a simple, common object starting from scratch and bypassing any productive mediation. The book includes transcripts of e-mails, correspondence, and telephone conversations in which the designer tries to design strategies to solve his production problems. He tries to convince BP (British Petroleum), the multinational oil company, to take him by helicopter to a platform to collect the crude that he needs to make the plastic carter for his toaster, baking it and mixing it with potato starch and "stealing" water from the Marquis of Anglesey. It is an example of a design marked by the semantic and creative encroachment that proposes itself as a system of broad reflection on the world, and the ungraspable condition of contemporary beings. A confirmation, then, of how design itself has no value, or if it has, that this value is compromised with the value of production processes, scale production, raw materials, marketing, and so on (Thwaites T., 2011).

1.3. Thomas Twaites "The Toaster Project", United Kingdom, 2009. Photo: Daniel Alexander.

In his own way, Thomas Thwaites reminds us that there is a design for luxury and one for survival, a design for injuring and for healing, design for oneself and for others, costly design and inexpensive design, a design at the service of governments and one for protest, etc. Design is malleable at will; it is a substance that can become a drug or a medicine very easily. Even better, design thinking is a capital, and like any capital, it has a different value depending on how it is used and the context in which it is applied. The purpose of this essay is to start from the contexts that generate the project, and not from the project itself. Then, the second step is reflecting upon the methodologies adopted, on the languages, on the outcomes, and on the relationships that the project is able to trigger.

In our society, we find ourselves more and more often designing for our survival or for the affirmation of the values that represent us. This is why absurd and speculative projects teach us just as much as the most utilitarian and functional projects, if you learn to read the processes and concepts before the results. And this is precisely what this book proposes to do.

Towards a Phenomenology of Value

"This music is like Detroit: a complete mistake. It's as if George Clinton and Kraftwerk got stuck in an elevator" (May D. cited by Shuja H., 2017). This is how Derrick May describes the nascent techno sound of the Motor City in the mid-1980s. The city is in decline, the great car factories have begun to dismantle and relocate production. This 35-km long strip of land inhabited by an African-American and Hispanic majority is marked with widespread pessimism (Toffler A. 1970). A new generation of young people is striving toward a dimension other than the sale or consumption of crack on the corners of deserted streets. They seek a redemption through which they might cultivate hopes for the future. Influenced by the theories of the sociologist-futurologist Alvin Toffler, three young African-Americans, Derrick May, Juan Atkins, and Kevin Saunderson, experiment with a music that "sounds like two intercommunicating computers. It has to sound like a technician did it. Here's what I am: a technician with human feelings." (May D., 2013)

This is how the redemption project was born, from illegal parties in the ruins abandoned by the industry: a restless entity, with a dark heart, genetically inclined towards innovation, which, over time, has evolved in a thousand ways. The first independent labels bloom, the young African-Americans come into play as DJs, inside and outside the city, traveling throughout Europe, creating a bridge with the nascent culture of English rave. Detroit is conquered by these new fervors. Techno becomes one of the most fascinating and most aesthetically successful examples of cyberpunk futurism, with a deliberately post-industrial sound that aims to erase the traces of the Ford-like sound of Motown, a record label linked in the imagination to something like Smokey Robinson and the Miracles singing "I Care About Detroit" (1968). It is a synthetic, digital music that looks to the future as something that already operates in the present, that emerges to overthrow an obsolete system. Techno embodies a vision of the musical project as *hyperstition*, a concept defined by the English philosopher Nick Land as an element of actual culture that becomes reality, through an imaginary mass functioning as potential that travels through time" (Land N., 2018). It is a vision of the future that intervenes upon the present. If projected onto the world of design, this concept restores an evolutionary vision detached from that baggage of conventions and stratifications that imprison it within a grid anchoring it only to industrial and material production. The project thus finds the natural tendency to overcome its limits, emancipating itself from a reductive and functionalist vision. This "techno" perspective embodies the work of the Akoaki Collective based in Detroit and coordinated by Anya Sirota and Jean Louis Farges.

O.N.E. Mile Project (2016) is the paradigmatic example of a design that stands as a collector of social value for the creation of a sense of community as a result of multidisciplinary collaboration. It is a project that brings about intense cultural activity in public spaces that are to be reinvented and transformed into places of experimentation, of practices that involve makers, artists, and creatives in general. They are places, therefore, in which to activate a neighborhood economy and to free relational opportunities. Akoaki's project has paved the way for a process of rethinking dismissed and abandoned spaces that, in agreement with the public administration, are generating a more extensive and inclusive vitality in the North End, one of the city's poorest areas. It all starts with the idea that:

> *"building the future means accepting the risk of consequences and imperfect solutions. You can always remain harnessed, but at least you have the opportunity to build new networks in which you eventually get trapped."*
>
> *(Srnicek N., Williams A., 2016)*

The project coordinated by the Detroit collective is a powerful tool for the transmission of new energies that can help to bring about spaces of action, of experiences and of new imaginings. *O.N.E. Mile Project* wagers on the idea that design can be a catalyst for change. This is why Akoaki designs objects, environments, and situations in which people can meet in an informal way, rather than being determined to develop new visions of public space. "Design does not stand alone, it is a contingent practice that needs a context, a program, but above all people. As a result, we plan activities and scenarios that emerge from a series of urban and cultural circumstances. Fortunately, Detroit's North End is an unlimited source" (Petroni M., 2016). It is a design initiative that is generating widespread attention from media and cultural operators. It is no coincidence that the 10th Design Biennial of Saint-Etienne (2017) has named Akoaki and Detroit guests of honor, in order to share the unique experience of a city that reinvents itself, starting from the rethinking of the conceptual paradigms linked to the value of design, and work more generally. Detroit has become "a prism in which to explore a new collaborative and sustainable way of living and thinking together. Today, the city boasts the highest concentration of designers in the United States" (Akoaki, 2017).

It often seems easier to design cities as grids within which to allocate social classes and tax revenues, rather than people and communities. But those same cities soon turn into spreadsheets filled with variables that generate errors in the management of resources. Often these numeric assessments lead to failure. *Out of site* (2017), Akoaki's proposal for the French design biennial, moves in the opposite direction of the cold, algorithmic calculation, focusing instead on the unveiling of a collaborative platform revealing how the inhabitants of Detroit are changing the paradigms of the relationship with work, through music, agriculture, and cultural production in general. Three of the urban installations created in Detroit are reproduced in Saint-Etienne. There, they host a program of activities curated by artists, designers, and architects, to continue the public conversation on the redevelopment of the city, in an attempt to overturn the depressed image widespread in the international imagination.

In Detroit, the capital of Michigan, some fascinating considerations of the Hungarian sociologist and anthropologist Karl Polanyi come into play. He looks at economics as an expression of the context in which we live. Economics is the way – never completely discounted – through which we respond to our needs and allow society to reproduce and find relationships with the surrounding environment. In this era, it is clear that we respond to our needs through market exchange, but the Hungarian author invites us to recognize other ways, which he calls "forms of integration." One of these is the idea of gift as economic behavior, but, above all, as a way to express our need for relationship, to communicate how and how much we want to contribute to the construction, maintenance, and strengthening of our relational, social, and cultural networks (Polanyi K., 1944). The movement "New work, new culture" was created out of this inclusive premise. It is linked to the rebirth of Detroit and to the ideas of the activist and philosopher Frithjof Bergmann (Bergmann F., 2014). It is a project of rethinking the city in order to abandon the miseries of the past and open up – without mediation – to the new possibilities of the present. This is a wager on new ways of thinking about and building Detroit, through cultural forms that are capable of granting centrality to the communities that dwell in it. It is a project of re-appropriation of public space, that passes from the sharing of places and economies, and is capable of not rendering people, relationships, and meanings superfluous. In this project, work hinges on inclusive enterprises that are naturally technological and intentionally social, productive realities that do not separate the subjective dimension from the objective dimension of work. These are places capable of building concrete opportunities for alternatives. Detroit is planning its escape from a system that has failed miserably.

We are experimenting with a social model based on these principles: design is at the center, an instrument truly capable of generating and holding together creative and productive networks, a call to new visions through a logic of proximity of common interests, needs, and perspectives. It is a dynamic and continuous evolution that represents a real laboratory of experimentation and production of new imaginations, through which the territory is transformed and made attractive while, at the same time, an enlarged, mobile, and open community is built. The lever that sets this system in motion is the search for a sense of inclusive collectivity, animated by processes of transmission of knowledge that are proposed as active contributions for the construction of a new sense of economic value. The engine of these proposals is no longer just free-market competition, but the desire to generate ideas, projects capable of a productive perspective, coupled with the use of knowledge gathered as a result of genuine practices of relational proximity. It is the start of re-thinking processes of economic valorization that, after debt and bankruptcy, allows Detroit to supersede neoliberal logic, putting people and ideas at the center. This complex system is driven by a spirit of survival and not of prevailing over others.

The Value of Community. A Conversation with Anya Sirota/Akoaki

The idea of transition has a central role in the vision of the revival of Detroit. Emerging within this evolutionary process are the contradictions of capitalism which, in that context, continue to express themselves in a violent form. In this way, design becomes one of the factors of transition, a form of searching for alternatives that are activated with the intent of returning the inherent dimension of uncertainty and creativity to the project. This is how the practices that are part of defining a turning point, a crossroads rather than a point of arrival, are created.

We met with Anya Sirota, the soul of the Akoaki collective, in order to deepen our knowledge of their design sensibility and to better understand the context in which they operate.

What is your approach to the public space and how would you define it within the O.N.E. Mile Project, one of the projects you are developing in Detroit?

Our work on O.N.E. Mile is the product of a powerful bond with the city: the identity of a place can be theoretical, projected, performed, constructed, made visible, even mythologized, and design can participate in the manifestation of symbols and synergies that work towards the greatest possible inclusiveness and social diversity. So, we imagined the creation of a public space as a scenario in precarious balance, one brought to life by events and networks that have a broad margin of instability. By combining the features of the setting, the legendary North End of Detroit, with a series of installations and cultural events embedded in the local context, we worked to investigate and renew the collective experience of a city endowed with many spaces — but of which few are public. In this situation, a public space is not a neutral amenity, but a place of expression, protest and validation.

An intense engagement with the translation of local attitudes emerges from your work. In this process, design is a crucial means of examining cultural connections that take shape in public installations, music and objects. Do you agree with this point of view? Can you explain the type of processes you have activated in the North End district?

The term "translation" is very appropriate. In our work, the research phase is lengthy, intense and really in a state of flux. We start by developing multiple relations with a huge network of cultural and intellectual producers, some strongly connected with the material reality of the space, others completely free. The aim is not complete consensus. Rather, this is about assembling and activating a critical, plural mass. Using this kind of operational framework, people can connect, design improvements, change and grow. The key process of the project lies in establishing a method of communication between a large number of actors who are not always in favor but ultimately share a series of political values.

Do you think that your design approach is connected with the real requirements of the local community? How do you identify those needs?

The situation in the North End and in many communities in Detroit is very serious: the infrastructure is decrepit, the public education system has been pummeled, access to water and energy is erratic, there are problems with healthcare, there is a lack of economic opportunities, and so on... These basic needs remain unresolved and are made visible by the absence of investment in the area. They are the consequence of specific social injustices that Detroit has suffered for many years. Design alone, unfortunately, does not have the force to answer these pressing social needs. What design can do is to create an environment for every single individual, a protected space where they can give voice to their own opinions, experiences, aspirations and problems, allowing us to modify the common perception of the city and reveal a multitude of stories that would otherwise remain hidden.

How are you working on your forthcoming participation in the tenth Saint-Etienne Design Biennale with the Out Site Project?

In recent years, Detroit has received the attention it deserves. It has been used as an arresting backdrop for numerous exhibitions, workshops and debates, and design experts have often employed it as the ideal tabula rasa for a series of experimental ideas. Faced with the curatorial task of framing this urban context in a new and frankly non-colonial way, my partner — Jean Louis Farges — and I laid down some rules. We aim to show projects one-to-one; that is, no models, drawings or prototypes, just direct translations. We want to deploy all the interventions in Detroit initially, and then send projects to the Biennale that are already "tested/completed". In other words, we privilege their evolution in the field and export them to deepen their effectiveness based on their real functionality. Lastly, we avoid working with scale projects, or with representations that show the citizens of Detroit as instrumental users. Instead, we want to treat the Biennale as an opportunity to raise funds and bring in as many as possible of the partners, performers, artists, farmers and urban activists who we have involved in recent years. The result is an exhibition that will occupy the central courtyard of the Biennale building with three large-scale installations, experimental music performances, and a cultural programme showcasing a multiplicity of scenarios and forms of professionalism adopted by Detroit. In the process, we hope to produce a commentary on the ways in which design can be employed beyond the normative relationships of capitalism.

You define design as a catalyst for change. To us, your work seems a social and economic platform for the local community. Do you agree?

It is a fact that change has emerged as a central battle cry and a mechanism for resistance. If change aims at the transformation of something, it does not imply at all that it will be for the better or for the common good. We have seen, for example, how Barack Obama's call for change was easily co-opted by the current government of the United States. For us too, change is a key word but not the final objective. We reflect and work on the will to absorb and reinvent standard models of urban regeneration so that people who are often excluded by the process can identify a platform for expression, if not for reconciliation with their context.

Your project is an ambitious one and opens up a space for new practices in design. What is your personal opinion of the design of the future, and how should it differentiate itself from today's design?

The projects that we have created as designers have deep political affinities, and inevitably they sustain values open to wider sharing. In the immediate future, design will continue to contribute, intentionally and otherwise, to current trends, reinforcing our entrenched social and political divisions. In Detroit, this takes the form of a confrontation between the aesthetic of a regime devoted to nostalgia and one more open to the future. Someone has said, in adoration of past industrial glories, that the city is geared towards "making America great again". But our view is that the encouraging thing about design is its capacity to create the desire to break the social bubbles generated by the algorithms entangling us. So, I hope to see design use its intrinsic ability to take the fullest part in public debate and in the political affirmation of a more inclusive world.

Could you tell us who benefits from your interventions and how? Has the area become more attractive? Were these your aims?

In economically depressed environments, design is often deployed to enhance the appeal of an area and point to its availability for regeneration. The idea that design can lead to gentrification and the involuntary transfer of people is not new. In the North End of Detroit, it is difficult to say whether we have improved the area's attractiveness. Many other regeneration projects are already taking place. We have definitely contributed to its visibility. The point is that this was one of the goals: making the cultural value of a place more visible by reinforcing its stories, from the African diaspora to its musical history, from techno to the birth of the Afrofuturism movement. We have learnt the hard way how this activity attracts attention from outside, bringing in economic investment too. Our projects also involve lawyers, economists, developers and sociologists. We have developed with them new models of collective ownership that secure areas and spaces to the advantage of local residents.

What is your goal for the future and how do you intend to improve your work in Detroit and abroad?

In her 2012 essay, "Artificial Hells: participatory art and the politics of spectatorship," art historian Claire Bishop hits the center of this problem through her critique of the practices of participation. The more we exploit art and design for social inclusion, the more we minimize our dependence on the state and the collective government. This is particularly worrying in the current political context, in which all of the social infrastructures in America seem to be under attack.

Sun Ra taught us recently that the linear notion of time is overvalued. The future is already here. We must tackle it now.

According to the philosopher Frithjof Bergmann, we are less free than we think, surrounded as we are by endless trivial choices. We will only be truly free when we have the chance to make our lives into what we really care about. Is there a connection between your projects and the "new work new culture" movement?

Frithjof Bergmann is the source of some original and influential reflections on new paradigms concerning the development of work and the community. We tend to agree with his negative reading of the financial renaissance, for example, admitting that the current scenario is not a recession and that cyclic Keynesian economic adaptation is part of the past. We certainly do not agree with some techno-utopists, who believe that the proliferation of 3D printers will free us. Our position is much less didactic than the "new work new culture" movement, which posits clear differences among creative enterprises, educated consciousness, and community building. We think that all these things are much more disordered and contingent, and that they often emerge from unplanned situations and cannot be systematically controlled. Let's say we are too romantic to align ourselves with Bergmann.

The right kind of design is a transformative and participatory activity that intervenes both on the individual and on society. Precisely for these reasons of modifications of the real, design is a process of production of often conflicting or resilient worlds. This is perhaps the key to understanding phenomena such as the progressive spread of community hubs, digital manufacturing laboratories, and coworking that is dedicated to social innovation. We are talking about spaces where we learn and share the use of new technologies, we rent a low-cost station, or we are looking for opportunities for autonomous and independent exchange. Very often this dimension generates a relational network of proximity that becomes the infrastructure and the sense of the project itself.

It is not difficult to understand, staying within the management of work typical of Taylorism or the autonomous exploitation of new platforms on demand, how a truly good project can never be realized. The organizational form must be that of the community that moves, decides, and produces in a horizontal way. We agree with Enzo Mari when he claims for the designer a double constitutive nature that, on the one hand, acts concretely on reality, and, on the other hand, imagines new worlds. "The first problem of a designer is to define his model of an ideal world, and not to create an aesthetic… The designer cannot fail to have his own vision of the world. If he does not have it, he is an imbecile who only gives form to the ideas of others" (Mari E., 2014).

Excerpt of an interview between Anya Sirota (Akoaki) and Marco Petroni, previously published on Domus web on 24 February 2017.

Chapter 2

Going With

"I mean, in the end we got used to it, but are we really sure it's a good idea?"

Submission
by Michel Houellebecq (2015)

The Exception of Value

27 January 2017: *Better Shelter*, the project coordinated by Johan Karsson, supported by the IKEA Foundation and by the United Nations High Commissioner for Refugees (UNHCR), won the Beazley Design of the Year Award for the best design projects of the year, awarded by the Design Museum in London. This is a residential module designed to replace the tents or other types of structures in the fields that are designated to accommodate migrants. It is made of recycled plastic, composed of folding elements and can accommodate up to five people. It features a solar panel on the roof. Production started in 2015 and, so far, over sixteen thousand housing modules have been sold in various parts of the world. The award has generated a great deal of media attention and quite a bit of criticism, mostly related to a suspected Swedish model of accommodation that uses this humanitarian operation to sponsor the world giant of furniture. Further, at the end of 2015, the Swiss authorities sent back sixty-five Better Shelter modules due to highly flammable plastic walls that make these structures dangerous, especially when used in enclosed spaces, very close to one another. These are the chronicles that show that migrants, a multi-ethnic, transient population made up of sixty-five million people, constitute the central issue of our time. Humanitarian policies and philosophical, economic, cultural and geographical visions all come into play in the understanding of this matter, with which we must necessarily relate.

The Dutch sociologist Saskia Sassen offers us an interesting methodological perspective by focusing on the fact that it is not possible to understand and eventually solve a general problem if we insist on thinking only about particular details. In her essay, *Expulsions: Brutality and complexity in the global economy*, she clarifies the relationship between physical and individual space, and analyzes the phrasing *"refugees warehousing"*, coined by human rights organizations. Sassen helps us to better understand the conditions of those who are part of a flow of people moving from one country to another, and that it is precisely because of this condition that they are deprived of freedom of movement for a long time and are forced to inaction in camps, reception facilities, or segregation. Hence, for migrants, expulsion does not consist solely nor simply of the impossibility of participating in the social and economic life of a state, that is, "expulsion from life projects, from access to the means of subsistence, from the social contract," but it is also a physical departure, a departure defined by precise geographical origins (Sassen S., 2015).

Saskia Sassen's analysis suggests that physical space is directly interconnected with social space, and thus paints a merciless, complex, international picture, which has been confirmed by recent economic and sociological research on the analysis of unemployment rates, on the consideration of the distribution of wealth, and on the number of people involved in migratory flows. The merit of her considerations lies in the invitation to look at these dynamics of expulsion as processes that create tangible spaces. "There are many, they are growing, and they are diversifying. They are potentially the new spaces in which to act, in which to create local economies, new stories, new ways of belonging." The result of these evaluations causes us to think of migrants as commodities that, unlike the globalization of products, do not enjoy the free market. We have broken down the borders for goods, but not for people. Despite the fact that their movements are the tragic result of nefarious political logic, migrants do not enjoy free trade. Whoever proposes to understand the problem of immigration must therefore analyze how, when, and why governments, economic powers, media, and the citizens of developed countries are involved in these processes.

Today, we tend to establish economic areas that are free from customs controls, on the one hand, and, on the other, to restore these controls in order to prevent migrants and refugees from entering. This is a vision that seems paradoxical in today's network of exchanges of capital, goods, information and culture. As governments and economic actors in highly developed countries seek to limit the role of state borders in order to create ever-larger transnational spaces (i.e. EU, NAFTA, ASEAN, OPEC, etc.), the contradiction between immigration policy and the trend towards global economic integration is clear. The coexistence of such contradictory systems is creating many difficulties in the European Union and in the governments of individual member states. *Universal Unconditional* (2015), a project developed by Stefania Vulpi, looks at this complex network of implications. The designer has created a web platform that involves a global community without borders, which continuously negotiates the concept of belonging to a state, making it elastic, flexible, and free from the idea of geographical origin. Quite simply, *Universal Unconditional* allows expats and emigrant citizens to donate their own rights, in the country where they no longer reside, to a foreigner living in that country, who, because of citizenship, does not have the same rights. In short, it is a worldwide network of people who temporarily exchange the rights attached to their citizenship. Clearly, belonging to one state rather than another can be a privilege, but also a limit. With the proper nationality, you have access to fundamental rights: medical care, the possibility of looking for a job, a home, and the potential to create your own future. The wrong nationality – or at least an unlucky one – implies tremendous limitations, the impossibility of crossing a border, or being condemned to poverty and wars.

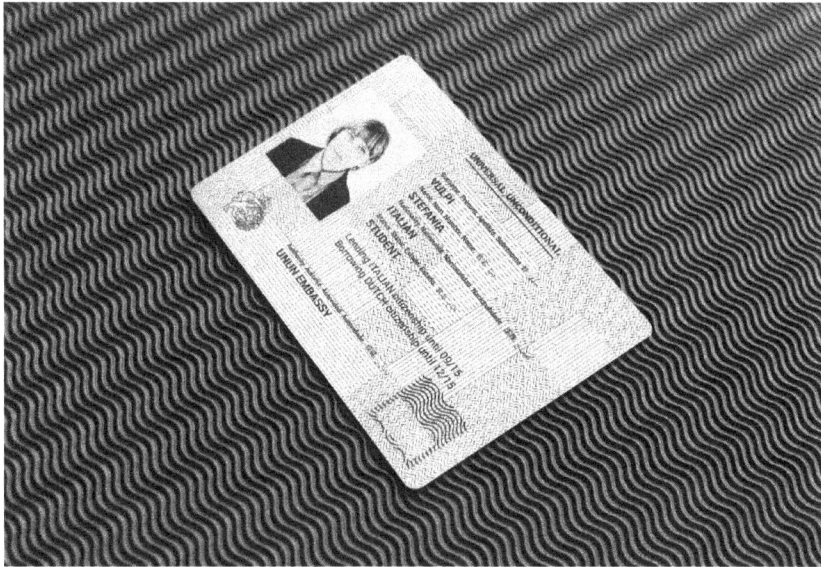

2.1. Stefania Vulpi "Universal Unconditional", The Netherlands, 2015.

Stefania Vulpi has hypothesized and created a system in which citizenship is a right that can be exchangeable and broken down into practical functions, such as the possibility of being able to leave or to receive free medical examinations. The members of the *Universal Unconditional* community are continuously immersed in the political overcoming of the limits and problems related to the current concept of citizenship that is understood as belonging to a state. Transactions take place on an internet site where you can register, indicate your nationality and what rights you want to transfer or acquire, and for how long. Once the transaction is completed, the system sends a visa, to be inserted into the passport, certifying the transfer or acquisition of the new temporary citizenship. "Geographical membership gives access to fundamental rights," says Stefania Vulpi. "The exchange would allow a foreign citizen to take his or her first steps in another country, to settle down, find a home and work. Once in good standing,

the person would no longer need the borrowed rights, and would return them."
The project puts in place a scenario that dynamizes the concept of citizenship
by intercepting and giving answers in terms of reception and integration. *Universal Unconditional* confronts us with the question: what are we truly willing to
share? In the so-called "sharing economy," everything moves in the direction of
an apparent collective use of goods, such as transport and food but, in reality,
Uber and Airbnb reaffirm an individualistic logic that capitalizes a desire for
sociality. The value of sharing arises, as Stefania Vulpi seems to suggest, from the
development of genuinely inclusive practices.

The project, *In Limbo Embassy* (2015), created by Manon van Hoeckel, is also moving in this direction. It is a mobile structure governed by asylum seek-
ers who, as ambassadors of a people and not a state, wish to engage in dialogue about their condition. The embassy stems from the necessity to respond to an elementary need for representation that refugees and migrants
often do not find in their own diplomatic offices, nor in the media. In this way,
the young Dutch designer has developed a nomadic device, a neutral meeting
place that travels among people in an attempt to create direct contact between citizens and migrants. The embassy offers an opportunity for dialogue,
confrontation, and cultural exchange on an equal footing, bringing to light
issues that are usually little known by the citizens with whom they would then
live. People who exist in this suspended condition without rights are often
subject to the impossibility of being able to return to their own country or the
inability to find a job or a place to rent.

2.2. Manon van Hoeckel "In Limbo Embassy", The Netherlands, 2015.

It is this state of exception that emphasizes how government organizations, more and more often, implement a suspension of rights because of world emergencies that determine an exceptional situation (Agamben, 2005). Projects such as this aim to bring out new spaces of action for design, attempting to establish connections, reflections, relationships with a world in which we witness the progressive growth and spread of violence and the growing loss of the ability to be supportive and cooperative. And so, while governments define geopolitics in which borders are becoming increasingly blocked to people and more permeable to goods, designers explore the interstices between borders. They create an ambiguous condition among that of citizen, expat, refugee, migrant. This approach, dedicated to the movement of people, partly clashes with the recent trends that designers seem to promote regarding goods and products, in which, on the other hand, the dogma of produce-local, consume-local is dominant. As if to remind us that local identities are defined by the resources of the place and how they are used, rather than by the nationality or the DNA of those who live there.

In the past, the response of governments has been the creation of blocks such as EU, NAFTA, ASEAN, APEC, which, created as economic agreements, have often been proposed as a hybridization between market and citizenship. The benefits deriving from the expansion of the areas from which to draw material resources – and therefore the concept of locality – are not, however, accompanied by critical pressures with respect to the concept of the border, which has simply been moved to the perimeter of the block rather than within it, nor to the concept of national identity. Governments have been unable to do much more than create imaginative flags and unlikely anthems to go along with these cross-national areas. Although the model represented by designers – that of the free movement of people and of local consumption – may seem ethically fairer, the risks that derive from it must be understood. A world in which resources are produced and consumed locally, while work moves according to the exploitation of these, is a world at great risk of conflict. These clashes would no longer be controlled by governments, but rather by those who control material resources and workers. That is, multinationals instead of nation states. In short, the utopias of designers are to be appreciated for their critical value, but they still do not seem to offer usable ideas. Unless you accept the risk of creating a dystopia.

James Bridle designed his project *Citizen Ex* (2015) in order to help us understand the sense of roaming, wandering, in the digital age. *Citizen Ex* is an extension for web browsers that allows our computer to keep track of all the different nations with which we come into contact during our daily internet use. *Citizen Ex* user creates a flag from all this information, which is an amalgamation of the different national flags of the locations of the servers that have been contacted (Bridle J., 2015). Thanks to this tool, we realize now that a customary act such as consulting websites involves equipment located in different, often improbable countries, with laws, cultures and economies that are totally different from those of the user. Thus, at the end of the day, you could end up with a digital citizenship composed of 40% USA, 15% China, 10% India, 10% Turkey, 5% Arab Emirates, and so on. James Bridle's work helps us to raise doubts about which economies we support during our digital roaming, about the impact that these countries' legislations might have on the information we access, or on the products and services we buy.

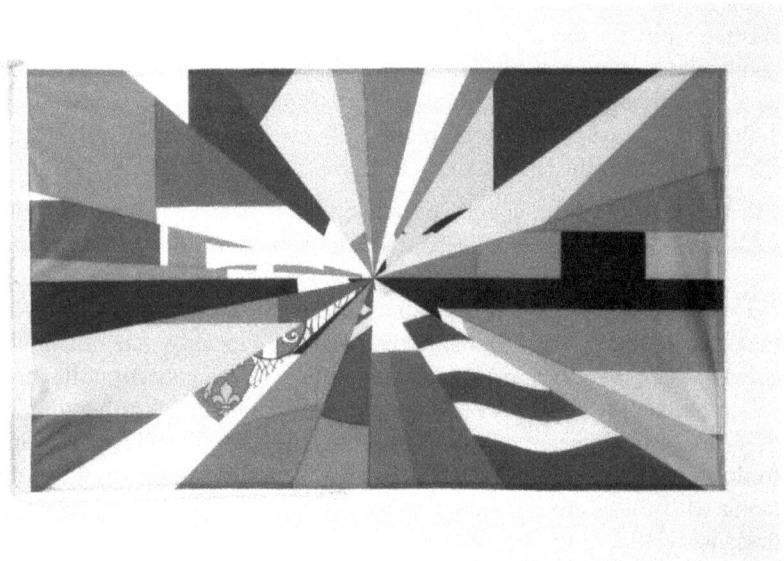

2.3. James Bridle, "Citizen Ex", London, United Kingdom, 2015 (courtesy of the Artist).

The Suspension of Value

In Idomeni, as in Ventimiglia, Calais, or Lampedusa, one lives in a suspended time – between the barrier that stands in the way of the future and the dramatic prospect of returning to the countries of origin. Walls, barriers, and police impose themselves like a lien on the present, but migrants are not the passive subjects of this suspension. On the one hand, many migrants choose the risk of illegal passage; while the other migrants who decide to wait, immediately resume the organization and production of their lives. Some of them build a dimension of everyday life through the activities that were familiar to them; others, in anger, may find a way to invest their energies in a petition to change the absurd procedure of the asylum application, to chronicle what happens, or to organize the network of those who want to get into Europe.

A self-organized dimension is created around a common problem, to break the selection that an authoritarian Europe tries to impose. This is the negation of the possibility to decide freely and actively about one's own life. At each border, there is a quota of those who are arbitrarily included, while others are separated and excluded. The purpose of this separation is the artificial creation of a stratification. The camp is only the first of a series of barriers, whose subsequent steps are found in access to citizenship, welfare, rights, and wages. Inclusion and exclusion become confused; they have a common sign given by the increasingly openly violent and hostile use of public force. Whether it is the violence of border clashes against migrants calling for the reopening of the border, or the arrests and the criminalization of volunteers and activists, the tendency is to manage conflicts by eliminating the possibility of dialogue in favor of police (or even military) control that is ever more stringent and oppressive.

There is a Schengen generation composed of all those people who grew up in the European area, within a narrative of the substantial dismantling of the borders, which today are recognized in the revindication of freedom of movement. This is a generation accustomed to being able to move for the most varied reasons, for whom it became a habitual practice, who grew up believing themselves free to move, not only because of their precarious situations, but also following desires and aspirations. The work and the construction of one's own subjectivity necessarily happens through movement. A freedom of movement within Europe that, in the last twenty years has constituted a line of flight, a possibility for the future. This mobile condition is not extended to migrants. In this contradiction of life, there is a large movement of young people. Through the slogan, "No Borders" – in Calais, Lesbos, Lampedusa, Ventimiglia, Idomeni, and also in Paris, Madrid, Barcelona, Athens, Rome – they give voice to a new vision of European territory, and beyond. The design activity of Marginal Studio of Palermo, coordinated by Francesca Gattello and Zeno Franchini, stems from these reflections. From an exploration of the concept of borders and limits, they try to define a design practice that continually questions the social role of design. Prototypes, installations, writings, films are the tools used to investigate and document public space, in close dialogue with other skills and cultures.

Marginal proposes design as a factor of constructive dissent to experience a necessary disciplinary rethinking, which is also a form of social practice and political awareness. *KHI-MI-KUNTI* (2017) was founded in Palermo as a proposal for a radical model of cultural and economic development that lays the foundations for the construction of a postcolonial *imaginarium*, inspired by

Hakim Bey's theories of *immediatism* (Bey H., 1994). The incoming migrants and a disintegrated industrial complex are the levers for imagining a new conception of local production and of renewed social structures. Through an informal network of craftsmen, present in diffuse areas in the Sicilian city, Marginal Studio is creating objects that are the result of a crossover, a cultural collaboration composed of local knowledge and techniques, with the participation of the African and Asian communities who live in or transit through the city.

Craftsmanship in Mediterranean countries has more in common than the individual processing techniques: their diffusion and differentiation followed the waves of migration and trade, bringing with them stories of oppression and encounters. Marginal Studio observes that migration is perhaps the most important cultural and social test that the Western world has to face today, a showdown of colonial relations that have occurred with the rest of the world through the past centuries. It is precisely this craftsmanship, which bears the traits of multicultural societies, that is preserved in an almost static manner, in an almost folkloristic way, rather than being lived and practiced as a social, cultural, and economic structure. In Sicily, cultural heritage is looked at with nostalgia, the value of what is left so immense that it becomes difficult to give it a valid perspective in the contemporary world. It is a design vision that digs into the folds of the real, intended both as a historical dimension and as an existential human condition of life.

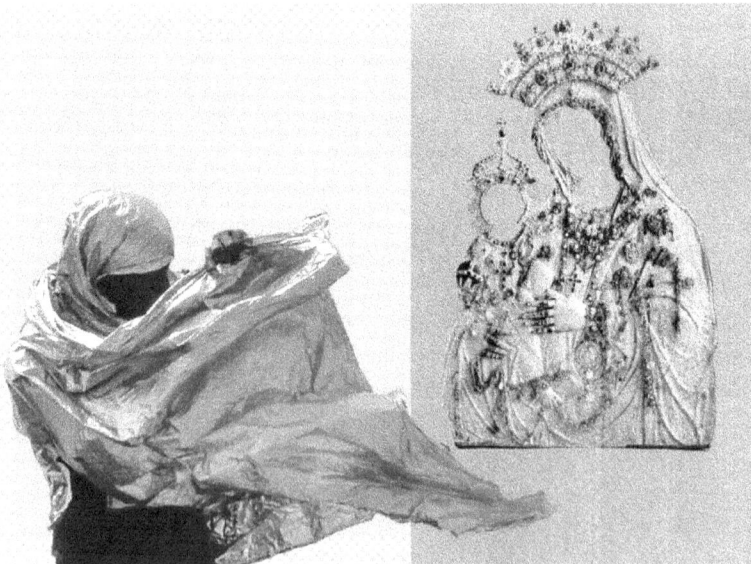

2.4. Marginal Studio, "KHI-MI-KUNTI, Palermo, Italy, 2016.

Everything moves in the direction of a renewal of the collective imagination, of an attempt to build a new common sense that reflects a world in profound transformation and the effects that these changes produce on the space of our everyday lives. It is about modifying our social imagination and reconfiguring the sense of what is possible. These projects are linked to the vision of value delineated by Paul Mason, in which design takes on the new task of trying to build a common language for a new world. Designers are called to claim a perspective that is not immediately feasible, but that must be designed and launched to grasp the operational and political possibilities offered by the scenarios of postcapitalism. A system in which knowledge, combined with imagination, constitutes the first capital to be valued. We are constantly encouraged to participate in the production process by bringing our culture and our experiences to the service of production itself, and to its incessant innovation. There is an inexorable difficulty in formalizing, and therefore measuring, this growing subjective involvement, so as to question the very notion of value that allows for the functioning of the capitalist mode of production. In fact, the work of the designer escapes translation and measurement in simple units, or it is not available in terms of calculable, quantifiable work. Every attempt to formalize it represents an impoverishment, and what is lost is the personal mark that is most interesting to capital. The designer objectively keeps the system in check by establishing that human activity is reduced merely to the production of goods created for the market.

The difficulty of working within capitalistic rules with the things that elude them because they do not have an objective value places the historical necessity, expressed by Paul Mason, of the transition to a plural economy, or of an economy that opens up to practices of inclusion, to other modes of subjectification that are not bound by an immediately quantitative evaluation. The current exploitation of the so-called general intellect, that cultural baggage prepared by an entire community in non-remunerative activities, unpaid and therefore devoid of exchange value, shows how the capitalist production system feeds on the predation of resources and design visions. Intelligence, culture, and creativity are a constant and growing object of monetization.

It is possible to think and practice a new concept of design's participation in the processes of redefining the world. The recovery of a radical awareness is at stake, in which the reflection of design's status as a discipline seems to be sterile. Faced with the cultural and economic dynamics of the contemporary, designers claim a social relevance with practices marked by transdisciplinary processes, and the value of its contents is conferred by a critical capacity of a reality that is able to challenge hierarchies and structures. We must welcome the invitation to get involved and to verify whether there is an intensity that produces the effects of transformation. Because of this, a reflection on the value of design and its contradictions is necessary. This is a need that is also shared by Beatriz Colomina and Mark Wigley, curators of the III Istanbul Design Biennial (2016), delineated as "an invitation to rethink what design is in our time. Our economy and our way of producing have changed so radically that we need a new concept of design. And the only way to find it is to expand the debate beyond the industrial design of the last 200 years" (Colomina B. and Wigley M., 2016). *Are We Human?* is the title chosen to link design to the profound reasons for its operative and reflective validity. "We need to gather the troops, because we are in an extreme, overwhelming and frightening world in which the old concept of good design is no longer very good. It's time to press the emergency button, which is extremely exciting," Colomina and Wigley assert. The ambitious show was organized in four main sections, called *clouds* (*Designing the Body, Designing the Planet, Designing Life and Designing Time*) hosted in several locations to give rise to a deep investigation around the sense of the human in design.

Various proposals have returned a dimension to design as an extended field with overlappings, references, and interferences interpreted by local designers and international stars who are also part of the contemporary art world, including Thomas Demand, Tacita Dean and Thomas Saraceno. An indicative example of the curators' vision and of their capacity to look into the folds of reality is *The Unstable Object* (2014-17) by Daniel Eisenberg, of Germany. This is a project of long-term observation and investigation on the conditions of production in the twenty-first-century factory. It consists of various videos that document specific factories, chosen as archetypes of structural, ethical, sensual, and economic relationships. Each one is different from the next. These portraits focus on the relationship between mass production and the individual. The video dedicated to the Ottobock factory in Duderstadt (Germany) is particularly effective. There, thousands of hand, foot, arm and leg prostheses are produced every day for the world market. From rural Africa to large international urban centers, from wooden feet to knees controlled by microprocessors, each object produced in this factory must be individually customized. So, by its very nature, Ottobock also produces one of the most advanced forms of individualized mass production. These prostheses are often designed to be as invisible as possible, but what remains most unexpressed and hidden are the causes of their proliferation. Landmines, wars, terrorist attacks, accidents at work, and medical amputations multiply each year, making prosthetics a steady growing industry. "The biennials have become a way to tell the world that all is well, and that design is healthy, but you're not really invited to think," Mark Wigley says. "We decided to accept the invitation to curate the Istanbul Biennial because we believe that investigating the profound nature of design is the most urgent question. Man is the only animal that designs, so it is for this reason that we can ask ourselves questions about humanity" (Colomina B. and Wigley M., 2016).

In light of the spirit that animated this interesting Biennale curated by Wigley and Colomina, design appears as an area in which it is impossible to define the object and the boundaries; it represents an attitude, an intensity that is activated in relation to art, architecture, economy, philosophy, poetry, desire, love – even to boredom.

Ettore Sottsass clearly grasped this dimension, affirming that design is similar to the wind or a storm. It produces, shakes, transforms and even destroys the place, the context in which it is applied, but, just as unpredictably, passes and disappears. This reminds us that when we talk about a project, we must re-member that there is a value in the intent, in the process, and also in the result. And each of those results needs to be assessed separately. The problem of de-sign education also comes into play, because, for a long time, only the act of designing was taught – not to imagine, nor to express a critical judgment. "If you have to teach something about design, you must first teach something about life, and you must also insist that technology is one of the metaphors of life" (Sottsass E. Jr. and Bill M., 1983). And so, despite the proclamations of those who want design to be a driving force of our society, it has remained at the mercy of what is happening around it. When we think of design as the sole agent of change, we should remember the case of Vespa, the scooter that arose out of the mechanical parts and the technical knowledge of the field of military aviation. World War II did not end because Corradino D'Ascanio decided not to design more warplanes and to concentrate on scooters, but the opposite formulation is true. That is, D'Ascanio decided to design the Vespa because the war was over (Gundle S., 2009). This teaches us that design is primarily a witness to change, and only then does it become a tangible manifestation. This does not diminish the importance of design, but it does give it a different role – that of telling about the world and its changes. The study and criticism of contemporary design help us to better understand the world in which we live.

"Design has become the world," Beatriz Colomina and Mark Wigley state. And to delineate the radical nature of the issue, they have developed *Super-humanity* (2016), an extremely fruitful editorial project in collaboration with *e-flux*, one of the most cultured and refined digital windows into the artistic culture of our time. Fifty reflections by writers, scientists, artists, architects, designers, philosophers, historians, archaeologists, anthropologists have defined an enlarged scenario of the design world in relation to "the human." In it, they answer the question: what forms of life are currently undergoing a process of design?

Thus, emerges a conceptual hypothesis that attributes a cultural centrality to design by relating it to other disciplinary areas. Franco Berardi "Bifo" relates it to political theory; Hito Steyerl, to the status of the image; Boris Groys to philosophy; Paul Preciado to gender theories; Spyros Papapetros to architecture (Berardi F., 2009; Steyerl et al., 2012; Groys B., 2008; Papapetros S., 2012). In many of these contributions, migrants represent the agent of transformation, capable of activating a continuous process of negotiation with urban and suburban spaces. Culturally and physically, the presence of such characters and their active involvement strongly change the social and cultural structures of the cities, generating the effervescence that Emile Durkheim saw as a fundamental element for the construction of a much more inclusive and innovative community. Design must update its operational and conceptual tools by focusing on improving practices that are capable of relating to various factors such as population structure, public behavior, and values that are diversified and transformed through a coexistence of differences.

The Formation of Value

There are events that inevitably force us to take a stand vis-à-vis with the complex reality of our time. These are border-situations, margins, areas in which a micro-universe of meaning is able to reflect almost all the issues at stake. This is the case of the violent eviction of the Jungle, a temporary, spontaneous city, experienced by migrants in transit from Calais to France. On October 24, 2016, the "humanitarian operation" of "cleaning" the Jungle with truncheons and tear gas began. Long metal barriers filter, regulate, and monitor the movement of the inhabitants of Europe's largest spontaneous settlement of migrants. Men, women and children, kids with luggage, backpacks, suitcases, and boxes are invited to get onto buses that are going somewhere in France, to villages, towns, or larger cities, the names of which most of the travelers discover upon arrival. Almost all of the bonds and relationships built during the stay in the Jungle are broken; only few manage to stay together. Others refuse to participate in the trip organized by the French Ministry of Internal Affairs, and stay put observing the agony of the Jungle. They observe the last moments of collective life and still they try to cross the Channel; they will continue to try to get onto the vehicles in transit. This is a humanitarian operation that is certainly not an invitation to a free choice to remain in France. The reasons behind the choice of police measures for the management of the migration crisis are a strategy to disperse migrants, leaving behind smaller groups that are easy to control. This is done to prevent the possible formation of numerically large groups that might generate conflicts or pressures, or even the development of support for migrants in transit. The dispersion and division are therefore aimed at neutralizing and defusing possible conflicts of migrants and control the space around them. A denial of identity and vitality. This is an obvious case of how the politics of consensus and fear is able to produce a contradictory dimension that deforms the characters of the phenomenon to the point of making them monstrous and potentially threatening. It is a widespread attitude that proliferates on various levels. In the universe of communication on social networks, we speak of algorithmic bubbles to indicate those devices that select and censor the content that we display via Google or Facebook. In politics, this has to do with the neo-reactionary and populist movements that, at the local level, label as dangerous any form of inclusion, multiculturalism, and, in general, the openness towards everything that is labelled as "external."

Calais is the synthesis of two extreme polarities; the local and the global. In both of these opposite scenarios, we can see how contemporary Europe is shaken by the eruption of unprecedented phenomena. In confronting these phenomena, in orienting themselves to this scene, a great fatigue has arisen, like an actor whose script seems out of sync with respect to the setting in which he must also be able to act. This condition means that we must develop a new toolbox to smother the surface of concepts in order to distinguish between those that are still usable and those that must be thrown away, without any nostalgia. We must identify some useful ways in which to inhabit the threshold between what is no longer and what is not yet. This is a widespread condition of the present time. In this sense, the reference to Postcapitalism delineated by Paul Mason offers the impetus to cross the edge over into the "after," in the search for those structures of planning and culture that can define the historical framework of the social transformations that are still in progress. We must try to nourish and sustain practices to renew an imagination that is reduced to the contrast between worlds and cultures, in order to open us up to what Jacques Ranciere calls "partition of the sensible," which is the ability to redesign the space of perception, making visible what was invisible before (Ranciere J., 2000). These are the spaces of conflict, according to Ranciere, that will open this possible revolution of the gaze. This is what happened in Gezi Park/Istanbul and during the Arab Spring, when generations of young people on the other side of the Mediterranean tried to change the status quo. Politics, like design, is then configured as a practice capable of changing the way we look, feel, and perceive the world. We must assess where the contradictions that will allow disrupting the existing status quo might arise.

The freedom to choose where to go and decide where to apply for asylum is a right that is neither foreseen nor granted. Rethinking asylum and protection, together with – and not as an alternative to – freedom of choice of movement and of existing is the challenge that the migrants' struggles ask us to live up to. "The least of the possible evils" is the logic to which the humanitarian register accustoms us. *The Refugee Project* (2014), developed by the New York collective Hyperakt and by the activist and designer Ekene Ijeoma, invites us to act and to fully understand the complexity of this theme. An interactive map reports the annual migrations of people from dozens of nations ravaged by conflict, famine, or repressive governments, from 1975 to today. Infographics are integrated with brief stories on the major crises that have caused migration over the last 40 years. The project draws from the data on forced migration collected by the United Nations; data are then visualized, but this information from the UN Refugee Agency (UNHCR) excludes, for example, those who have become refugees due to natural disasters, the large numbers of those who migrated for economic reasons, and displaced persons in unlisted countries (Hyperakt and Ijeoma E., 2014).

Political persecution often occurs at the periphery of the globalized world, and victims cannot always report to UNHCR authorities for registration, but above all it is not in their interest to do so, since migrants are often unwelcomed guests, confined to reintegration camps, politically impotent, and they are often denied the rights to work and to expatriate. *The Refugee Project* emphasizes how new conflicts break out and humanitarian crises multiply, while existing wars remain unresolved. It is essential for the world to overcome its differences and find political solutions that can prevent and stop wars and famines. The project confronts us with the possibility of a new understanding of the problem of migrants. It is an invitation to empower humanitarian workers, governments, academics and citizens to seek solutions for the most vulnerable people on the planet. The project allows us to recognize the numerous stories of the many migrants who can be found in every part of the world. These stories can contribute to the creation of a gaze that can go beyond the gathering of different people under the common denomination of "migrants", opening up to the different motivations of their escape and focusing attention towards their individual circumstances. *The Refugee Project* was premiered at the exhibition, *Design and Violence*, curated by Paola Antonelli at MoMA in New York (November 2013 – May 2015). It is an online exhibition that has delineated the ambiguity of the concept of violence and its representations in the design world. The museum's curatorial concept is connected to the constant confrontation with a complex and constantly changing reality in which the theme of migrants takes on a central value. This is a complexity, as described by the American philosopher Wendy Brown in her interesting essay, *At the Edge: The Future of Political Theory*, that is generated by the lack of clarity in the boundaries that delimit the political realm, starting out with those that separate the public, private, cultural, and social spaces (Brown W., 2005). People's doubts about the certainty of boundaries, and the consequent impossibility of drawing maps, is the cause of a sense of disorientation to-

wards the present. Wendy Brown sees an opportunity in all of this. It is a matter of overturning a situation in which this loss of references became a pretext
for an attitude of impotence and resignation. It is exactly this sense of frustra-
tion that populist parties exploit.

For designers, the current situation should be a challenge for redefining the
very boundaries of the discipline, including questions, objectives and themes
that have never been previously contemplated. Also, theoreticians and critics
continue to stimulate change in the real world and can no longer afford to
remain anchored to static and institutionalized identities. Such a bond would
nullify the very sense of making theory; that is, transforming one's point of
view to the world. If design over the past twenty years has been characterized
first with its multidisciplinarity, and then with its interdisciplinarity, the appeal to contemporary designers is to adopt *undisciplinarity* as a spirit and
method of work. Working in an *undisciplined* way means not adopting notions that come from various fields, but instead, daring to criticize and refute
some of them. The notions of value, cronyism, and rights can no longer be
borrowed from what industry or politics propose. The project of our time
consists precisely in redefining these notions, rather than applying them.

The research of the collective Parasite2.0 fits well into this scenario. It car-
ries on an attitude of continuous investigation of the geographical and disciplinary boundaries and a redefinition of the contexts in which design operates. Recently, they have developed an interesting research project: *The desert
on the margins is my heimat: for a non-eurocentric vision of migrations* (2016).
The project looks at the camps in which migrants live in transit in Europe and
in the world as islands marked by profound radicalism. The camps are interpreted as places of collective experimentation, in which the condition of the
border suggests a rethinking of the concept of migrant. Everything starts from
these borders, where new communities are formed in the continuous traffick-
ing of an everyday life, in which everyone tries to affirm his or her own subjectivity and cultural codes. Migrants are immersed in a dimension of constant negotiation with the places they pass through, and where they are often
obliged to stop. They are always forced to establish new imaginative and operational relationships with the world. It is a difficult condition, full of obsta-
cles fueled by the incessant search for an identity that brings sense and signif-
icance to their existence. In this constant practice of mediation with the
world, Parasite2.0 see the passage and multiplication of a postcolonial sense
of being migrants (Parasite2.0, 2017). The project starts with a reflection of
Edward Said who indicated the migrant as the key figure of the twentieth
century. In Said's view, the migrant is a kind of liberating, homeless, decen-
tralized energy whose conscience is represented by the intellectual and the
artist in exile; or by a political figure who is placed between multiple territo-

ries, between multiple forms, between several homes, between multiple languages (Said E., 1993).

2.5. Parasite2.0, "The Domestic Promised Land: the desert, the net and the bones", Rome, Italy, 2016. Photo Credits: Operativa Arte Contemporanea.

Recent economic and social dynamics have erased the exceptionality of the nomadic condition, making it the only possible way of affirming one's own subjectivity in a context of perennial global crisis. This is how an identity of culture and design is created, as a process of transformation, of redesigning the world. The value of design is activated in many directions, in an area of continuous transit between cultures, and social and individual stories (Petroni M., 2016). As Chicano poet Gloria Anzaldúa says: "Living on the borders, in the margins, keeping intact one's own multiple and ever-changing identity, is like trying to swim in a new element" (Anzaldúa G., 1987). Parasite2.0 indicates a lateral, non-Eurocentric point of view on the issue of migrants, using the Jungle of Calais – that's how the migrants' settlements are referred to – as the most representative case in which, in the face of a fundamental human rights violation, small, self-managed schools and service systems arose, supported by activists and volunteers. Parasite2.0 invite us, however, not to ascribe excessive radicalism to these situations, to avoid mystifying them through rhetorical theories.

In this context of overcoming the humanitarian vision, it is worth noting *Refugee Heritage* (2016), a project of the Palestinian collective DAAR, Decolonizing Architecture Art Residency. This is an attempt to redefine the value of migrant experiences beyond the narration of suffering and constraint. Unlike cities and countries, refugee camps are built with the intention of being demolished. They are the paradigmatic representation of a political failure; they are destined not to have history and future. They are destined to be forgotten. The history of the camps for migrants is constantly erased, rejected by states, by humanitarian organizations. The only story that is recognized within migrant communities is that of humiliation. But the camp is also a place full of stories told through its urban fabric, spontaneous activities, human relationships (DAAR, 2007). In tracing, documenting, and revealing this multiplicity of experience, *Refugee Heritage* tries to define and practice a camp dimension that projects beyond the humanitarian approach, trying to contaminate the spaces dismissed by the cities and to negotiate the right of residence in a place that is not a tent or a temporary shelter. It appears necessary to start developing theoretical and design tools to break the boundaries of multiple cultural, political, and social bubbles. There is a need to give back a centrality, a value to a world of design that seems increasingly distant from common sense. Victor Papanek taught us that the center is the community and its life, understood as a communion of biological, social, and ethical life. It is therefore important to focus again on the culture of the communities, whether permanent or in transit, so to undertake a task that we believe is collective and currently imperative (Papanek, V.J., 1984).

Chapter 3

Going In

"Do you think about the future? How will you come back? The body will be the same, certainly, or strengthened; but the mind? Will the conscience remain unaffected? Will you be the same person?"

Zero K
by Don DeLillo (2017)

Towards a Biopolitics of Value

The forms of government in which we are immersed are complex and stratified projects. Democracy is perhaps the most complex, or at least the most problematic, of all. We are trying to design a way out of a system that, in many ways, fails miserably. The obvious signs of this decay can be summarized in two concepts: control without a controller; democracy as an algorithm. The two concepts are fundamentally linked to each other. The lack of a controller derives from the inability to hierarchize the agencies that should regulate our societies and, consequently, our lives. National governments, trans-governmental organizations (EU, ASEAN, NAFTA, etc.), corporations, all exert pressure on each other and superimpose their power. In this confusion of hierarchies and roles, decision-making is delegated to formulas and algorithms, data and statistical forecasts. This brings us to the second concept: democracy is an algorithm.

But what is an algorithm? And how have they transformed our way of producing, communicating, knowing? Tracing a hypothesis of analysis of the change in the perceptual and identity paradigms produced by algorithms is a fundamental theoretical basis for understanding the profound implications that this transformation has within contemporary design. The body intended as a battlefield is placed at the center of all frictions, to delineate the complexity of the scenarios we are facing. In industrialized societies, we live in a triple condition: as citizens, consumers, and free people. This subordinates us to three forces – social good, market logic, and free will – which sometimes operate harmoniously, with a common purpose. However, often these three forces come into conflict with each other, creating frictions and tensions. These conflicts are often amplified, activated, or resolved with the use of more or less advanced technologies. Never before has technology had such a great influence on the human body. And never before has the relationship between the human body and the surrounding context been subjected to control that is so extensive and meticulous. We can choose to freeze our sperm and eggs, so that we may work now and dedicate ourselves to family at a later age; we can analyze hormonal harmony to find our ideal partner; we can emigrate to countries that tax saturated fats. We are in the constant situation of making choices to define who we want to be and to what life we want to live. At the same time, those who offer us these options ask us to support or associate ourselves with their interests.

Our bodies are a battleground at the intersection of ethics, politics, economics, design, and science. To govern this intricate relational system, there are algorithms, a digital calculation tool of more or less important probabilities that are at the basis of our existence. The stated goal of this method of governance is abstraction, the dematerialization of the subjectivities involved in the dynamics of everyday life. "Contemporary capitalism has evolved along two main vectors of abstraction: monetary abstraction – financialization – and technological abstraction – up to the algorithms of society metadata" (Pasquinelli M., 2014). Reading the publication, *The Algorithms of Capital: Accelerationism, machines of knowledge and autonomy of the municipality* (2014) can help to understand the ambiguity of these processes. Edited by Matteo Pasquinelli, professor of media theory at the University of Arts and Design in Karlsruhe, it is a dense collection of essays that tries to investigate the folds of those abstract machines that are at the apex of the production pyramid and that, today, manage every component of the division of labor, of communication, and of the logistics of market goods. To understand how an algorithm is designed to process data generated by the user, think of how social media or Google works, or the distribution logic of Amazon or Walmart, or software capable of predicting crimes. An algorithm collects preferences and habits, and carefully balances this data based on who the users are, where they are, when it is activated. Algorithms are democratic processes because they work on the concept of majority, applied ad hoc. That is, at a given moment, in a given place, the majority of users with a given profile, would like *X*. It is a *smart* version of consensual democracy. In this dimension, we can count three agents competing for our choices, our bodies and, finally, our lives: governments protect the social good by promulgating and imposing laws and rules; corporations pursue their economic interests through the products and services they offer us; and finally, there is our free will, which aims toward self-determination and making decisions independently.

One of the obsessions of our contemporaneity is the collection of data, even if we must recognize that we have always tried to classify, count, and describe the information relating to categories of people in an orderly manner. Historically, populations have used censuses to organize themselves, to give themselves an order that should serve the management of cities, territories, and the division of property. Once the calculations were made and the names and ages of the actors involved were recorded, the rulers could determine how many men were suitable for war, for work, or how much land there was per each household. This need, therefore, has always existed: it is a primary necessity for social control, an instrument through which order can be guaranteed for any social form. With the advent of metadata companies – or Big Data – we are witnessing an evolution that sees our own network of relationships become a technology of control and a basic productive factor of the economy of our time. Silicon Valley is the epicenter of these tensions. The capitalism governing this community, with one of the highest densities of designers in the world, bases its own power on its algorithmic mastery in manipulating data and information, creating "an area in which the body in its entirety connects to technological devices in such an intimate way that they enter into a symbiosis in which reciprocal modifications and simulations take place" (Griziotti G., 2016). Our network of contacts and the way we interact with them becomes the fuel that feeds the algorithm that governs us. The information is no longer transmitted by state television, but by a Facebook friend who shares an article. We are the medium. And the message? Knowledge and information are the raw materials of this system, which amplifies a process of hybridization in which bodies and technologies intertwine and open themselves to the dimension of posthuman, well theorized by the philosopher Rosi Braidotti. The identity of the human being, in light of technological progress, is undergoing a profound change (Braidotti R., 2013).

It is necessary to understand the nature and the sense of these new scenarios in which the individual appears as a set of fragmented data, useful only for capitalist extraction of value, and how today these phenomena are taking shape in an acritical climate, especially in the world of design. In *Make It New. A History of Silicon Valley Design*, for example, there are many interesting points for reflection. The author, Barry Katz, reports on the birth of Apple's global vision by linking it with something that Steve Jobs said: "I want our design to be not only the best in the personal computer industry but the most effective in the world" (Katz B., 2015). Only thirty years later will we discover that the most effective design in the world configures a new economy – the sale of digital goods to general public – and a service – that of absolute privacy – that clashes with our governments' policies of security and control. This statement from Jobs is from 1982. The same year, a number of Apple managers organize a trip to Europe to meet the designers who can possibly realize this ambitious goal set forth by Steve Jobs. In London, they meet with Pentagram, one of the largest design studios in the world, a powerful, multi-branched multinational of industrial consultancy. In Paris, they meet Roger Tallon, a whimsical French designer and engineer who was very prolific in the seventies and eighties. In Milan, they interviewed Ettore Sottsass, who started the Memphis project and collaborated with Olivetti, where Mario Bellini works. Bellini declines the invitation to meet the Apple team, so as not to incur dangerous conflicts of interest. Out of these meetings comes the idea to start a competition to choose the designer who will be assigned the development of new products. A small German studio, Esslinger Design, participates in the competition. This studio grew up in the shade of Dieter Rams, the well-known designer of Braun electronic products. Hartmut Esslinger's studio won out over the other, more famous competitors by proposing the integrated office station *Snow White*. This is an interconnected system of smooth, candid white plastic that combines into a single element a fax machine, a screen, a PC, and a telephone. "The clean, clear lines are the synthesis of a way of giving a cultural expression to a new technology," says Esslinger, "simple, white, innocent, sexy and a little bit more radical" (Katz B., 2015). It is a decisive step, a paradigm-shift in the world of product design. If Raymond Loewy embodies the American path to functionalist modernism, the German, Esslinger, takes a leap forward by championing a vision embodied in the claim "form follows emotion." This led to the creation of Frog Design, a design corporation at the service of the nascent *new economy* of Silicon Valley. Its major clients are Hewlett-Packard, Atari, Sun Microsystems, Apple. Esslinger travels between Germany, Japan, California, and England, where he selects talented young people who are able to give shape to his post-functionalist vision. He goes to the Royal College of Art in London, home to a nascent course of Interaction Design, the ideal place to choose designers such as a very young Ross Lovegrove, Stephen Preart, and others. These are the prerequisites for the construction of a system based on the idea that desire and emotion are needed to produce machines that are capable of insinuating themselves into society and revolutionizing it. Design collaborates in the construction of *desiring* machines that shape the digital revolution. And thus, opens a new era in the expansive logic of capitalism. It is necessary to accelerate economic transactions and to focus on the dynamism of information, its economy of *desire* and its state of *perennial crisis*. All are ingredients that push towards digitalization, automation, engineering of the human body and artificialization of the planet.

Gilles Deleuze and Felix Guattari had seen the power of these clues in their seminal 1972 essay, *The Anti-Oedipus. Capitalism and schizophrenia*. "Always one machine coupled with another... The synthesis of production, the production of production, has a connective form: and, and then... Desire lets flow, flows..." (Deleuze G. and Guattari F., 1983). In this dimension of flow, design has lost its attachment to reality by carving out an accessory role, at the service of the capital. In this post-Fordist scenario, in which there is ever greater evidence of the dematerialization of work, the growth of the service sector, the centrality of all sectors of care, culture, sociality, and education, the design world has preferred to embrace a cosmetic logic, abandoning its role of a stimulus of reality. It is a condition of service without any critical push with respect to the profound transformations that are asserted in a model of cognitive capitalism based on the need to invest in the knowledge and definition of new imaginings.

In this scenario, creative work acquires a contradictory centrality. It is in this passage that we can see the crisis in value creation, which is not only a change of the processes of production in Fordist terms, replaced by temporary labor, externalization, outsourcing, and crowdsourcing. But it is a crisis of the role that design can play in these profound transformations. This passivity has certainly produced a relapse in terms of loss of opportunities. A more trusting hypothesis would include a necessary definition of a subjective measure of the value of design that refers to the possibility of making choices and is generated by what we want and by what we know. That is, autonomy and resistance, as an alternative to the "measure" imposed by Silicon Valley corporations. This is an invitation to design critical tools, which are necessary not to succumb to technological power. In order to do this, it is necessary to build a network of vigilance or opposition towards the cultural passivity induced by the globalization that is governed by the Californian model.

The Life Fair: Welcome to Post-Contemporaneity

Bio-techno-bodies immersed in continuous media communication. Almost a trap. Everything is caught, everything lives in the network. Everything exists only in its *mediality*. Digital commodities. Our bodies are no longer a two-dimensional surface onto which power, law, control, and desire are imprinted, but rather a knot in the network in which life takes place. A new corporal, medial, ever-connected subjectivity emerges. The combination of advanced capitalism and biogenetic technologies generates a perverse form of fluid and nomadic subjectivity.

Every human interaction is caught in the gears of the global economy. Life itself is the fundamental capital. Globalization involves the commercialization of planet Earth in all its forms, through a series of interconnected, highly automated and algorithm-controlled appropriation tools. A scenario full of contradictions opens up in front of us, proving that capitalism is very quick to detect and exploit the opportunities created by the decline of geopolitical balances and the consequent processes of cultural hybridization induced by the globalization of markets. This era, which was invented and managed by man, is referred to as *Anthropocene*, according to the definition created by Paul Crutzen – Nobel Prize winner in chemistry (Crutzen P., 2005). This theory, delineated in the 2000s, refers to the great acceleration of human impact on our planet. Over the years, many have embraced this line of thought. Not us, though. We think that there is a need to introduce a new "post-", an "after" that is able to break the ordinariness of the succession of events. What a bore, another "post-"? Yes, if *Anthropocene* is the era of the man who changes the world, *post-Anthropocene* is the era of the man who changes himself to adapt to the world that himself has compromised.

Post-Anthropocene provides the possibility for man to modify his body. This means that we can now monitor and improve our body. When we say that "we can change" our body, obviously we mean that someone else can change our body, since the knowledge and the technologies necessary to intervene upon it cannot be the prerogative of single individuals. In this way, our body becomes penetrable by other agents, thus becoming a market where governments, companies, and organizations at various levels fight for a place alongside – or in place of – our free will. A similar reflection to the one about *Anthropocene* and *post-Anthropocene* must be made regarding the transition from Capitalism to post-Capitalism. Capitalism has changed the economic systems and ethical values of the societies that surround us. Capitalism has replaced common good with the individual quest for economic capital and private ownership. The post-capitalist phase, which many identify as anarchism and/or socialism, presents a change in the values of capitalism itself, rather than a replacement of the capitalist model. Signs of this evolution are already evident. The companies that best represent capitalism are already gearing up towards new development scenarios. This evolution will see corporations oppose governments no longer just for economic reasons, but also on ethical grounds. The ethical and moral values of our societies are, in fact, the definitive commodity for trade. After the attacks in San Bernardino, California, Apple explicitly stated that the individual privacy of its users comes before communal security. This declaration generates an objective discrediting and mistrust of the American government: Apple establishes a set of codes and ethical values that are above the ones of the American government. A capitalist company becomes a replacement for the government, no longer just to defend its business agenda, but to provide asylum and protection to its users, to defend their rights that are put at risk by the government to which Apple should be accountable. Here, postcapitalism manifests itself as a Constitution, a code of ethics superior to that of the government. A Constitution to which we sign up whenever we log in to the technological device, accepting its terms and conditions. And so, we move from being American citizens (or any other nationality) to being citizens of the iCloud. Companies in the technological field (Apple, Tesla, Facebook, Google, etc.) create an alternative society in which they offer – according to their saying – more protection for the environment, for security, for the social ethics of equality, for our rights, than what governments do. And these companies are ready to confront governments for us.

Just as *post-Anthropocene* is opposed to *Anthropocene* because of its ability to change man himself and no longer just the environment surrounding man, in a similar way, postcapitalism ceases to have an impact only upon commerce, but also changes its rules by taking on the traits of a *super-governmental, para-governmental socialism*. In this scenario, we need to make choices about where we stand among the opposing forces of social ethics, economic profit and our personal satisfaction – we could even call it happiness. Article I of the Italian Constitution states that "Italy is a democratic republic, founded on work." Work is what makes us part of the Italian state, and, in a certain sense, it is what qualifies us as citizens. In fact, working is often one of the activities that satisfies us the most and makes us feel socially useful. So, what will happen when our work is done by machines? This is a banal question, one that arises from the time of the first industrialization. On a social level, the answers have been given with policies that should protect those who lose their jobs or who do not work. The surrounding community, in theory, takes responsibility for those who do not have jobs, and supports them by paying for their basic needs. Working citizens are taxed so to gather the resources that allow society to compensate for these problems. But if the workers are no longer people, but machines, then the taxation system must be radically rethought. The most provocative – and maybe also the most realistic – proposal in this direction is to tax the machines, the robots. This proposal was endorsed by Bill Gates, someone who knows about machines. This solution could support another very controversial proposal in industrialized countries, namely that of *citizenship income*. Taxes derived from robots would help pay for this social expenditure. These proposals open particularly interesting scenarios that undermine the concept of citizenship in the economically richer countries. First of all, we have to figure out how to tax the machines. That is, will robots be responsible to their country of origin (where they are manufactured) or to the country where they are put into use? A German-branded robot that is employed in China, say: will it have to produce tax revenue in China, Germany, or both? And then, how should the robot be taxed? Will it be a one-time fee, a periodic fee regardless of how much it's utilized, will it be taxed for the actual work time, for the operations it performs or for the products it produces?

One notices immediately that every answer to these questions could lead to different types of robots and, consequently, through different products. There could be very fast robots if we decided to tax the time of use, or you could have very unrefined products, if we chose to tax the number of mechanical operations it performs. Moreover, the robot that pays taxes transforms itself into a social actor that must be protected. Similarly to the worker now, the robot that does not work tomorrow will be a social problem. As a matter of fact, we will remain subjected to production and, therefore, to consumption. Here is how the income of citizenship enters into our discourse. A hypothetical income of citizenship reinforces the citizen-consumer model. That is, the civil responsibility of the individual will be exclusively that of consuming and no longer working. Objection could be made that consuming and working are two similar activities. In fact, consumption produces information about what we need and what we like. It would not be so bizarre to imagine, in the future, an artificial intelligence that automatically generates new products simply on the basis of what society consumes.

Returning to the Constitutions of our governments, if work is no longer necessary, we must also reconsider the principles that constitute a country. In this, the *American Declaration of Independence* seems to be a step ahead of other Constitutions. By stating the fundamental right to the pursuit of *happiness*, the American Constitution does not propose work as a way to establish citizenship. The pursuit of happiness can take place in any way, including, in fact, consumption. The first paradox of postcapitalism is the inversion of roles between governments and corporations, with the latter, which will (and already do) represent and protect individuals more than governments do, which will create *para-state* nuclei with their own constitutions and rules. In fact, this represents a social-capitalist structure. The second paradox that characterizes postcapitalism is represented by the new conditions of a salaried citizen as the consumer, and a robot that pays taxes and thinks. This involves a shift in the relationship of man-machine subordination, with the machine that acquires social value, and that we will have to support in order to guarantee tax assistance to our community. Finally, postcapitalism forces us to rethink the role of work in our existence as a citizen. Working will be superfluous; it will become an activity that is more personal than social. We could work at Starbucks for two weeks simply to get a taste of it, and spend our time on something else.

If the role of governments has often been to get us a job to make us function within in the social system and to make us feel personally satisfied, now governments will have to help us to look for happiness elsewhere. Traces of this new role of work are to be found in high-tech corporations such as Facebook and Google, where some employees are free to change tasks and hierarchical position, or to take long vacations and sabbatical periods while still contributing to the knowledge and the operation of the company. This is possible thanks to the role of automation and artificial intelligence, which are capable of updating and sometimes innovating production and economic system without continuous human intervention. Soon, designers will have to deal with the design capabilities of machines, with artificial intelligence that will not "steal" our jobs, but that, rather, will expand the spectrum the design process. Technologies have always expanded the field of creativity, and artificial intelligence will do the same, extending it in two directions. On the side of *absurdity*, generative design adds the possibility of an absolutely random association of ideas and inspirations that our brains cannot generate. While on the side of *rationality*, artificial intelligence allows us to include in the project an infinite series of factors and variables, offering us a wider range of logical solutions. Designers will have to carve out a role that is increasingly outside of the strictly design process. For example, designers could play a more crucial role in drafting the network involved in their projects, in establishing relationships for the dissemination and marketing of the design. In practice, designers will act more and more as a bonding element between the various actors involved, introducing non-quantifiable factors such as trust, intuition, charisma and critical sense into the design system.

The exhibition *The Fear of Missing Out* by the artist Jonas Lund (2013), comes into play when thinking of these matters. All of the works in this show are the result of a predictive algorithm written by Lund. Analyzing a wide range of works of art by established, contemporary artists, the algorithm has generated a series of instructions that explain, step by step, how to realize artworks with guaranteed success. Thus, the artist is left with the sole tasks of realizing and signing the works by following the instructions provided by the artificial intelligence he trained.

3.1. Jonas Lund, Cheerfully Hats Sander Selfish (The Fear Of Missing Out), 2013, coconut soap 7 min 50 sec video loop (courtesy the Artist).

Obviously, these are only embryonic forms of what we can expect from the future. The co-author of this book, Giovanni Innella, and Agata Jaworska have reflected on these and other aspects in their exhibition entitled *The Life Fair* (2015). A dialogue with the curators follows.

Let's start with the title. Why this choice and how did the idea of the exhibition come about?

The Life Fair mimics the format of a trade fair, with different booths occupied by governmental and non-governmental organizations, companies, artists and designers. Each of these exhibitors offers a solution, a choice of life. It seemed appropriate that the title of the exhibition would clearly anticipate the content. We wanted to avoid emphatic titles and the dialectic of marketing, leaving that kind of rhetoric to individual exhibitors.

The fair is organized into nine sections: Identity, Health, Sex, Love, Birth, Consumption, Work, Safety and Death. The exhibition stems from the desire to reflect upon the role that our body has taken on in contemporary society and economy. Our body is the territory of conquest for commercial, political, and social entities that, for various reasons, claim access and control. Social security, economic interests, the desire for self-determination are the forces that come into play whenever we make life decisions, creating conflicts with ourselves and with others.

Is it a biopolitical project? How do you include design into the scenario you have planned?

The exhibition is not a biopolitical project per se, but it includes many projects, products, actors who operate in the sphere of biopolitics. There are numerous exhibitors offering solutions that involve changes in the body, genetic control, or defining new configurations for family units and alternative ways to identify our ideal partners. We can implant chips in our body to open locks, we can choose the sperm donor based on his resemblance to Hollywood stars, we can think about marrying ourselves, we can do DNA tests comfortably

from home to know which genetic diseases we are likely to contract, we can freeze our body after death, hoping for a future cure that will bring us back to life…

Each of these solutions is obviously designed, even if not by designers as we conventionally imagine them. In the exhibition, design was evident not only in the proposals of individual exhibitors, but also as a superior presence. With the slogan of: "The Life Fair, where the life you want to live is waiting for you", the exhibition communicates the illusion of being able to live as you wish, but then it unveils a system of agencies to which we subscribe each time we choose a product, a service, a party, or an organization.

What are the curatorial lines that you have delineated in the exhibition project?

The curatorship of this exhibition is made following the direction taken in a series of previous exhibitions that Agata Jaworska and I have curated in Germany, China, and Qatar, with the title of Domestic Affairs. We try to include content coming from architecture, art, consumer products, speculative design, but also statistics, news, services, organizations, brands… Our goal is to represent the changes in our cultures with an ethnographic and general approach, rather than one that is specific and technical. In The Life Fair, we also tried to include content of fundamentally intangible nature.

For example, we included the saturated fat tax that the Danish government applied between 2011 and 2012. We did this by exhibiting a kilogram of fat and a statement about its corresponding tax revenue. We came up with other exhibition solutions for Cosmetic Surgery Travel, a travel agency that combines holidays in Southeast Asia with convenient plastic surgery services. In their stall, we included graphics with photos of patients on holiday and the silicone implants that are used in surgical implants. Or further, for an American NGO that fights against the death penalty, we chose to broadcast a voice that reads the actual last statements of those condemned to death.

The result is an exhibition that is difficult to label as design, art, or something else. Probably calling it an ethnographic exhibition would be the most correct definition. Thanks to the diversity of the content, the exhibition recalls the stream of posts that fill our streams of posts on social networks. Just as on our Facebook walls, where important news, daily life, hoaxes, the most intimate aspects of our lives come together without a predefined hierarchy, also in The Life Fair there was no distinction between "high" and "low" content, between intellectual debates and popular culture.

Cryogenics, subcutaneous chips, and others are some of the archetypes de-lineated in order to define a world that is dominated by bio-economics (from bio-mimetic to synthetic biology, up to the recent research on bio-sensors), a system that combines cognitive capital, technological innova-tion and generative and evolutionary capacity. Why do you think it is nec-essary as a designer and curator to reflect on these issues?

We believe that one of our roles as designers and curators is to seize and anticipate the cultural, political and economic changes in our so-cieties. At this moment, bio-economy is one of these and we are inter-ested in exploring it and manifesting it for the public. We want to offer the public an opportunity to reflect, using the cues that the market, politics, and subcultures already offer us.

Isabelle Stengers, Donna Haraway, escape the narrative of Anthropocene that sees in Homo sapiens the cause and, simultaneously, the remedy for the ecological catastrophe. Do you also think that this is a reductive vi-sion of the issues at stake in the contemporary world?

We are not very interested in identifying the causes of the ecological situation we are facing. Instead, we are fascinated with understanding what kind of society is configuring on the horizon. It is true that many of the critical situations that we are facing are caused by environmen-tal catastrophes, but the solutions could be found not only in the eco-logical, but also in the cultural realm. The road to be taken may no longer be trying to minimize our impact on the environment, but to change the impact of the environment on our body. This could be achieved by intervening on our body, perfecting it, accepting ourselves as the architects of our evolution. In a certain sense, by accepting that we can no longer just be Homo sapiens, to live in the world that we ourselves have transformed. And also, that we cannot afford waiting for the time it takes for Darwinian evolution to adapt our bodies to the new environment. In this passage, we will have to continually redefine — in addition to our body — our culture, society, and economy. In an embryonic form, The Life Fair attempts to summarize some of the exis-tential dilemmas that we should pose or that we are already asking ourselves. As curators, Agata and I tried to draw from reality, trying to limit the use of fictional speculative design. This is why 70-80% of the content of the exhibition is represented by actual products, compa-nies, policies that are already available in different parts of the world.

In the exhibition you have given an important space for the technologies of social control. Why this choice?

This is a decision that arises from the desire to understand, to investigate the forces that allow a society to determine itself, to control itself and eventually to subvert the systems of this authoritarian determination. Technology introduces the concept of agency, which is a third entity between the individual and the government that can change the existing balance. Take the case of Apple, which prefers to preserve the privacy of its customers as opposed to the security of society, as an example. Technologies of social control, are the same technologies used to escape such control, just used in a different manner.

One of the themes that emerges from your project is the transformation of labor. How do you see this question in the design world?

We need to rethink the concept of work. In a context in which data processing is delegated to machines, data production becomes crucial. Artificial intelligence is increasingly in need of large amounts of data to operate and develop, and providing that data is a form of work. Each of our online searches, every purchase, but also the use of devices that monitor our home activities and health conditions, represents a basic form of work. The consumer and the user have become the working class of our industry, they are the laborers of data production. With their decisions, they automatically inform the material production processes that in turn will have fewer and fewer workers.

Millions of cognitive and creative workers such as engineers, designers, philosophers, and artists have produced the innovations that transform our lives. What is your stand on the fact that a world marked and drawn by intellectual and creative work corresponds to a constant impoverishment of the role of the designer, not only in economic terms?

The design critique that has very often celebrated designers who work on now-marginal products such as furniture and crockery certainly holds some responsibility for this. If Facebook changes its interface, or if Google changes its search algorithm, it would be opportune to analyze and comment on these changes, from a technical, cultural, and even aesthetic point of view.

Who designs the interfaces of the services we use every day, and how and why? Or further, is there an aesthetics of laws, of ethics? Why not analyze and comment upon electoral voting cards or political campaigns, under the lens of design? And shouldn't electoral laws be assimilated to service design? I believe that at least in part, what design is and what's the designer's job has been defined by critics. If the discussion of design included fewer design celebrities, perhaps actual designers would be able to access roles that are more crucial in our societies.

3.2. Agata Jaworska and Giovanni Innella, "The Life Fair", Rotterdam, The Netherlands, 2015. Photo by Johannes Schwartz.

Giovanni Innella and Agata Jaworska's words about *The Life Fair* resonate with another experimental exhibition curated by the well-known Chinese artist and activist, Ai Weiwei. This is the *Biennial of Gwangju* (South Korea) of 2011, entitled *Unnamed Design*. An exhibition thought as an antidote to the market's fixation on showing recognized and established designers, who are themselves an added value. In fact, Ai Weiwei decided to include a pamphlet that was distributed in Tahrir Square during the Egyptian uprising, with advice to protesters on the most effective tactics for civil disobedience, including how to make an improvised helmet and how to break the lines of police control, and further, a series of drawings for IEDs (Improvised Explosive Devices) of the kind that kills the troops daily in Afghanistan, a video of plastic surgery with the competitors from the reality show *Ultimate Fighting Championship*. In a long article published in the Guardian, Justin McGuirk wonders if all this represents design, or if it has anything at all to do with it (McGuirk J., 2011). The answer is that it would be very difficult to argue that these elements are not designed or do not encompass aspects that refer to design itself. The collective behavior, bombs, and extreme organs all require a design. Rather, the exhibition curated by Ai Weiwei raises a reflection around all of the rhetoric that circulates in the claim "designing a better world" that is implicit in so many contemporary productions. Projects like *The Life Fair* and *Unnamed Design* do not just lead in the direction of the well-established, now widespread enlargement of the field of design, but above all, they invite us to look beyond the objects to understand the ethical, economic, and political systems that produce them.

Is Design Everywhere?

Critical writing is a specific practice, capable of leaving signs and traces that cross a hybrid and unstable territory populated by processes of recompositing all those political, sexual, cultural components that refuse or do not submit to the dominant logic. Following this perspective, design is proposed as the education of a gaze that activates a change, not a repetition of what exists. It is an attitude projected into the contradictions of our time and opposes all those forces that want to reproduce reality as it is, without transforming it. In the face of these determinations, the value of design frees itself from an unequivocal, quantitative measure to become involved in a relational multiplicity that is fed by the transmission of hybrid knowledge. It is an opening onto the world that becomes a critical strategy of subjective affirmation. Manfredo Tafuri invites us to project our gaze and thought onto "the many languages that make up the real," having clearly understood that "the product of history is a crisis, a rupture, a separation, a decision" (Tafuri M., in Assennato M., 2016).

   In this scenario, design practices relating to public space are understood as the epicenter of the economic, social and cultural tensions of those who pass through and live in it. An example is the project *Silence* (2016), an interesting experiment developed in Beirut, which starts from the precariousness of urban space threatened by various factors such as land speculation, noise pollution, the constant fear of attacks. A group of students of the American University of Beirut, coordinated by Rana Haddad and Joanne Hayeck, tried to stimulate a change in the fruition of the urban dimension of the Lebanese capital. As Rana Haddad explains: "In Beirut, life goes on day-by-day, without anyone knowing what will happen tomorrow" (Petroni M., 2016). The perception of an uncertain and unpredictable future defines the necessary and transitory nature of the project that is shared through continuous comparison with the concept of borders. The city with its inhabitants constantly experiences an existential laceration between those who suffer it and those who wish to overcome it. Recently, the philosopher Remo Bodei has dedicated an essay to the subject. In it, he affirms that "it has become urgent to rethink the idea of borders, whose full awareness has been lost in part so as to be better able to define the extent of our freedom and to calibrate the range of our desires" (Bodei R., 2016). Precisely starting out with the rethinking of the idea of borders, intended not as a constraint but as an authentic possibility of construction and therefore of design, *Silence* takes a look at Beirut in an attempt to propose new ways of sharing urban life. The city in its material and immaterial dimension is imbued with economic, religious, ethnic, and political relationships that make Beirut a paradigmatic example of urban contemporary space, in which it is possible to measure oneself in a condition that is, at the same time, both exhilarating and distressing.

Four installations in different parts of the city give shape to a system for exploring the metropolitan sound space, activating a complex pedagogical system that aims toward the horizontal involvement of the students and the communities of reference. Gefinor Plaza, Rue Spears, a noisy, busy street near the headquarters of the Ministry of Cultural Heritage and the National Library, a highway bridge with a pedestrian crossing near the City Mall, and the Horsh park are *Silence*'s sites of convergence and analysis. *In between* is a walkway in wood and metal that stands out from the ground of Gefinor Square to project itself into a dense frame of branches and leaves that define an isolated and solitary viewpoint onto the city. Although the square represents a space of suspension in the dynamics of metropolitan traffic, the noise dominates and cancels the beneficial effects of a break. The ramp that cuts through the square leads the user to momentarily detach and reflect upon a new space, a sort of nest made of leaves that muffle the noises of the outside, letting the wind blow through.

A buffer zone of urban decompression in which, silencing the outside, one lays down a condition suspended between the silence of nature and daily activity. *Tazahor Mashrou* arises from the observation of a modernist building threatened by demolition mandated by the Ministry of Artistic and Architectural Heritage. Designed by architects George Rais and Theo Kanaan in 1950, it is located on an extremely busy road. The denial of permission to develop a part of the project within the building suggested the realization of some words written in Arabic under the portico, which signal to the community critical issues in the perception of the urban space. The multiplicity of meanings of the words *Tazahor* and *Mashrou* in the Lebanese language has given rise to a series of articulations of meaning, small points of information that punctuate this part of the city. *Tazahor* can mean demonstration of protest or demand, unveiling; *Mashrou*, on the other hand, is design in the Arabic language but also an apparition, a schema, a regulation. An invitation to reflect on the meaning of these words in everyday practice, trying to break through the distracted and passive transit through the city. Thus, the project tries to improve, involve, and question the urban dimension by reacting to the widespread passivity of the inhabitants of Beirut. "Silence is a pedagogical tool," says Rana Haddad, "both for the inhabitants of the city and for the designer, and emphasizes the importance of the subtilty and transiency, also bringing into play socio-political issues."

Aiming to educate our scrutiny and activate urban observation points, *Sma la Farjik* – "Listen to observe" – is the installation that insists on a pedestrian bridge that was chosen by the students because it is particularly noisy and uncomfortable. An urban element that crosses a highway, but without providing adequate access to the inhabitants to reach a bus stop that is essential for getting around the city. The users of the bridge expressed their discomfort to the students, who were there to understand how to develop a project capable of satisfying the wishes of the community that crosses it. The near-uselessness of the bridge and the paradoxical denial of its function led them to think of a box into which each passerby can insert his head for two or three minutes. A momentary isolation from the surrounding noise, to which a message is added to the outside and inside of the box. Like ostriches that bury their heads in the sand, pedestrians can read: "there is hope" or "there is no escape", or "you can make your voice heard." Twenty-two wooden boxes spread along the pedestrian bridge invite passersby to stop and listen, to modify the use of this apparently useless portion of the city.

The final installation directly addresses the theme of the border: located in one of the most controversial places in Beirut, Horsch Park, bombed and burned in 1982 during one of the many wars that flagellated the city. This is an area to which, until recently, access was forbidden. Now access is limited only to Saturdays, while another portion of the park is open every day. The two parts are separated by a metal gate. *Silence* connects the two parts through the creation of a playful element: a swing installed directly on the gate invites people from both sides to play together. How to redefine a border? How to overcome it? With a smile. Children, of course, were the first to jump on the swing and to clarify how any border is not impassable. Clearly, a game that breaks down a wall or a border frightens the authorities, who, considering it too dangerous, asked the authors to dismantle the installation. Examples of a social way of looking at design, combining the formation of a look upon the city with the search for new spaces of action for contemporary design.

3.3. Mario Khoury, American University Beirut, "Silence", Beirut, Lebanon, 2016.

The project *Refusal Party* (2016) also looks at these implications. Marco Petroni – coauthor of this book – developed this project with Martina Muzi as part of the *Consuming the Social* debate, curated by Jan Boelen in Eindhoven, and in Ljubljana for the *XXV Design Biennial*, curated by Angela Rui and Maja Vardjan. It is a process of crossing different urban contexts that are capable of stimulating reflections upon the transformations that are taking place around labor and its value in the world of design and beyond (Muzi M., Petroni M., 2017). The body, in relation to the many forms of work, is a privileged area for investigating urban spaces. "Beyond the immaterial change of our daily landscape, we are faced with a technological complex that forces us to deal with the need to fight the denial of access to reproductive and pharmacological tools, to environmental disasters, economic instability, as well as dangerous forms of unpaid or underpaid work," says the collective Laboria Cuboniks in *The Xenofeminist Manifesto* (Laboria Cuboniks, 2014). *Refusal Party* brings into play performance practices related to workspaces through the encounter with different situations and realities. It reveals an attitude to design as a tension anchored to the real world, to everyday life, and at the same time tries to indicate the unexplored dimensions, contradictions and paradoxes of our time. *Refusal Party* opens up a space of criticism and induces a perturbing experience with respect to established certainties. Investigating the close ontological relationship between design and daily practices leads to the definition, or better, to the search for a political form that is determined bottom-up, activating the differences in contexts and material and immaterial conditions that cooperate towards a mutual strengthening. It is an operating enclosure of a form that has not yet stabilized. Thanks to this hoped-for reunification, design practices suspended between reality and possibility become an interesting territory of investigation. *Refusal Party* defines itself in this suspension as a practice that, only through the creation of a group of bodies, and through the occupation of a more or less determined space, puts itself in the condition of creating some form of resistance, some form of capturing a different time and a different kind of work. It moves through questions and real passions, aiming to build a singular look at the world, as part of a struggle for autonomy.

We must think in order not to be thought of by others, if we do not want to limit ourselves to living according to categories that we refuse and which, too often, appear as traps. Projects like *Silence* and *Refusal Party* remind us that protest can be a flourishing and reflective planning ground, proposing thoughtful alternatives to the format of marches, shouted slogans, and vandalizing hackings. Both projects work by subtraction: *Silence* subtracts spaces from the negligence of the public administration, and *Refusal Party* creates a reduction of time (or work) from the capitalist systems and gives back space and time to the individual. They are projects that work much more toward the affirmation of a nomadic and fluid subjectivity, rather than for a specific community. Thinking and acting with design, therefore, means opening oneself to a precarious, complex operating condition that connects bodies and machines. In this process, one does not limit himself or herself to portraying of the existing, but instead tries to make a transformation on reality.

Afterword

by Angela Rui

It isn't exactly as we had imagined it.

Not so much the *future*, which we struggle to imagine, but the *present*. The *present* is a time that we still struggle to embrace, under the fury of continuous epochal changes, always tremendously new. We could enable the *present* only by accepting a different development of the *future* to what was projected by the generations before us. In attempting to understand what has happened and is happening to the design world in the reality (hallucinated and very true) that this book describes, we cannot avoid telling what is happening to us all. We find ourselves surfing very quickly over the surface of the planet and its apocalypses with a constant sense of guilt for not contributing effectively to an immediate change, which is necessary for improving the reality that is given to us. The true challenges we face are not future events that we imagine or dismiss with apocalyptic scenarios of sci-fi destruction: they are real trends. Data indicate that much of what we fear for the future (the collapse of the economy, the depletion of oil, global warming, and wars over the hoarding of resources) has already begun (Rushkoff D., 2013). In the totalitarian global order of the speculative financial capitalism under which we live, the media are constantly bombarding us with information concerning reality, but this information is primarily a planned deviation, distracting our attention from what is true, essential, and urgent. There is much information about what was once called politics. But politics has been supplanted by the global dictatorship of speculative capitalism, with its merchants and bank lobbies.

Another chapter of the information with which we are bombarded focuses on the *spectacular*: on shocking and violent events, wherever they occur, all over the world. Robberies, earthquakes, shipwrecks, insurrections, massacres. Once shown, one *spectacle* is replaced by another, devoid of context, in an expressionless succession. They are presented as *shocks*, not as stories. They recall the unpredictability of what can happen and show the risk factors inherent in life (Berger J., 2016). And in being *shock*, they affect the subject, giving him the impression of being a participant subject. A collapse of content, an inappropriate use of the notion of individual responsibility, and the failure of a possible shared and collective form toward which the sense of civic duty should move. As Pierre Bourdieu argues, the contraction of the social world today is perceived in the form of a personal drama. In noticing the lack of an orchestrated, programmatic, proactive look by the institutions, already, at the beginning of the 90s, Bourdieu was pointing at a return to individualism. A sort of fulfilling prophecy that tends to destroy the philosophical foundations of the social state and, in particular, the notion of collective responsibility, which has been a fundamental achievement of social and sociological thinking (Bourdieu P., 1998).

As the authors of the book point out, *Neoliberalism* has thus become the form of our existence – the way in which we are led to behave, in relating to others and to ourselves. It is not just politicians, business leaders, the media elite and academics who have been enlisted in this worldview, but also workers, students, migrants – and everyone else. In other words, *Neoliberalism* creates subjects. We are built as competitive subjects – a role that embraces and surpasses the productive subject of industrial capitalism. The imperatives of *Neoliberalism* bring these subjects to constant self-improvement in every aspect of their lives. Perpetual education, the omnipresent need to be employable, and the constant need for self-reinvention are all pieces of this neoliberal subjectivity. Furthermore, the competitive subject straddles the division between public and private. Our personal life became as competitive as our professional life. Under these conditions, it is no surprise that anxiety proliferates in contemporary societies. Indeed, an entire set of psychopathologies has been exacerbated by *Neoliberalism*. Stress, anxiety, depression, and attention deficit disorders are increasingly common psychological responses to the world around us (Srnicek N and Williams A., 2016). Every year there are 800,000 suicides globally, and every second, Twitter is flooded with people telling the world that they want to die. Designer Keisuke Fujita Makes explicit the weight of the social drama that is consumed in the social network with his installation *Voltaic Realism* (2017). A tiny device connected to a large block of coal scratches 0.0054g of material to each tweet announcing a suicide, the energy footprint of every tweet. A scratch is almost imperceptible, but hour after hour the material that falls to the ground makes explicit the collective drama. *Voltaic Realism* is an existential machine, sharing the perception of an uneasiness that today has a social dimension, and not only an individual one.

4.1. Keisuke Fujita, "Voltaic Realism", Eindhoven, The Netherlands, 2017.

Here is another interesting fact in the evaluation of this dimension of reality. To assess the impact of major economic crises, we can look at the relationship between unemployment and suicides. Between 2000 and 2011 the relative risk of suicide associated with unemployment increased from 20% to 30% in all countries (Nordt C., et al., 2015). It has also been made clear that job insecurity is now everywhere: in the private sector, but also in the public sector, which has dramatically increased the number of temporary or part-time positions; in industry, but also in institutions of production and cultural diffusion – education, journalism, the media, etc. In all of these areas, this insecurity produces more or less the same effects, which become particularly visible in the case of the unemployed: the deconstruction of existence – which is deprived, among other things, even of its temporal structures – and the consequent deterioration of the whole relationship with the world, time, and space. Such uncertainty prevents irrational anticipation and, in particular, the belief in and hope for the future that one needs in order to rebel against the present conditions, even the most intolerable ones (Bourdieu P., 1998).

There have been proposals for forms of resistance against the homologation of the post-capitalist system which takes possession of our existence. They range from the individual resistance that is exercised in making oneself invisible to the world, through ploys that avoid identity recognition (just think of all the projects that insist on the theme of surveillance); to the belief that a

small, healthy, local, and possibly self-sufficient system can completely replace the political need to build a wide and programmatic sociality. This is an
error that the contemporary political left has been reiterating for some time
through horizontal movements, which are based on stemming discourage-
ment and pessimism, causing the contraction of a planetary movement for a
better future. And then, there is the attitude of renouncing, typical of new
generations which do not consider resistance, thinking instead that doing
nothing is itself a form of resistance. This type of "collective mentality", common to all eras, is the source of demoralization and the loss of militancy. The
unemployed and the part-time workers have suffered a severe blow to their
ability to project themselves into the future, which is the precondition for all
the so-called rational behaviors, starting from economic calculation. In order
to conceive a revolutionary project, in other words, a motivated ambition to
transform the present in relation to a projected future, one must have a certain sense of mastery of the present. This means freeing ourselves from the
decrepit economic image of humanity that capitalist modernity has instilled,
and inventing a new humanity.

But how?

The latest wave of automation is creating an era that is historically unique in
many ways, including drastically changing the distribution of the labor market, even as it encompasses every aspect of the economy: data collection
(radio frequency identification, big data); new types of production (flexible
production of robots, additive production, automated fast food); services (AI
customer assistance, assistance for the elderly); decision-making processes
(computational models, software agents); financial allocation (algorithmic
trading); and, in particular, distribution (the logistic revolution, self-driving
cars, container ships, and automated warehouses). In every single function of
the economy, from production to distribution, from management to retail, we
are witnessing large-scale trends towards automation (Srnicek N and Williams
A., 2016). Emancipation under this vision would therefore increase the ability
of humanity to act according to whatever its desire may become. In this sense,
the possibility of an economic world capable of acting in full automation
must be directed towards the possibility of universal emancipation.

The ambition underlying the pages of the book is to rescue the future from
capitalism and to build the twenty-first-century world that we want. Perhaps,
by providing the time and money that are fundamental to any meaningful
conception of freedom. The traditional battle cry of the left that requires full
employment should therefore be replaced with a battle cry that requires full
unemployment. But let's be clear: there is no technocratic solution and there
is no need to progress to a post-labor world. The struggles toward full automation, a shorter workweek, the end of an ethic of work, and a universal basic

income are mainly political struggles. The post-labor imagination generates a *hyperstitial* image of progress – one that aims to make the future an active historical force in the present. The struggles that this project will have to face require that the left go beyond its political-popular horizon, rebuild its power, and adopt an expansive strategy for change.

> *Ne*
> *travaillez*
> *jamais*

Rirkrit Tiravanija (2016) began to disseminate this message at the beginning of 2000, but few understood what the artist admonished, associating the message with his participatory art. "Never work", he said, spreading the message that twenty-two-year-old Guy Debord had written on a wall in rue de Seine in 1953, the first symbolic act of a political (and aesthetic) uprising against the established order and the soft comfort of France of *Les Trente Glorieuses*. With commendable anticipation, Tiravanija sensed what the danger would be in the years to come; probably the intentional proposal to create works that are situations, where the encounters happen because the work creates them – as in the exhibition *Tomorrow is the Question* (Stedeljik 2016), in which he installed numerous ping-pong tables at the Museumplein in Amsterdam, with the aim of provoking encounters between people, in a dimension of non-progressive involvement, but of pure leisure. That should be read in the ensemble of its configurations as a unique act of resistance to the unquenchable request for efficiency and success to which the individual is constantly subjected.

Then, in a world in which the occupation of human beings cannot but diminish, if we decide to embrace a utopian vision, at least this time, of a world to come in which reality will not only be what is conveyed by the media and its shocks; if we are capable of resolving a constructive and shared critique to reactivate a true political conscience of a Social State; if we are able to remove the individual point of view, and see that every great narrative of the twentieth century – from capitalism to communism, from Protestantism to republicanism, from utopianism to messianism – depended upon the faith that held it up; if we are able to accept anti-hegemonic strategies, and if, and only if, we manage to move to the immediacy of a post-historical reality, we will be able, in that condition, to make sense of existence.

In recent years, we have often wondered what the role of design was. We wondered why we saw, in design, for example, a large number of exercises and currents digressing from the resolution of the urgent issues that we confront each day. We wondered why there were all those *useless* projects, and sometimes, too, we were angry. Probably designing lascivious behavioral forms has its reasons, and it is not useless. It has to do with a great new challenge, which is to plan the *new* time that – in the not-too-distant future – will be available to us. It has to do right to laziness, non-suffering, pleasure and fun; to a different use and occupation of time, and to a different form of self-realization, if that will not occur through work. And all of this has to be imagined on a global scale, through the planetary redistribution of resources and wealth. In the end, all we are trying to do is move as many human activities as possible into a phase in which we decrease the labor that is necessary to support a rich and complex human life on the planet, and, in turn, increase the amount of free time. And in the meantime, the boundaries between the two will have faded even more (Mason P., 2015).

About the Authors

Marco Petroni (Galatina, 1970) is a lecturer at Politecnico di Milano, Università della Campania Luigi Vanvitelli and Accademia di Belle Arti di Napoli. He writes fine arts, fashion, architecture and design in international magazines about. Marco is also a member of the international research group Design School: The Future of the Project, supported by London Design Museum (UK), Lancaster University (UK) and Charles Sturt University (Australia).

Giovanni Innella (Torino, 1982) is a designer, critic and curator based in Chicago where he is a Visiting Artist. Giovanni also occupies the position of an Assistant Professor at the Advanced Institute of Industrial Technology (Tokyo Metropolitan University). In his career, Giovanni exhibited at the International Design Biennale of Saint-Etienne and the Triennale Design Museum of Milan among other venues. His work is part of the permanent collection of the Stedelijk Museum of 's-Hertogenbosch (The Netherlands).

Craig Bremner is a Professor of Design at Charles Sturt University, Australia. For some time he was a Professor of Design at the University of Southern Denmark. Prior to this joint position he was Professor in Design Pedagogy at Northumbria University UK, and Professor of Design at the University of Canberra, where he was also Dean of the Faculty of Design & Architecture. He is a Director of both the Ecology of Care Network (a UK Community Interest Company) and a design consultancy in France. He is a signatory to the Lancaster Care Charter (2017) and his most recent publication, co-authored with Paul A. Rodgers, is DESIGN SCHOOL: after boundaries and disciplines (Vernon Press 2019).

Angela Rui is an Italian curator and researcher based between Milan and Rotterdam. She recently co-curated *I See That I See What You Don't See* - the Dutch Pavilion at the XXII Triennale di Milano (2019), as well as the 25th Design Biennial of Ljubljana (2017) and the accompanying book, both titled *Faraway, So Close*. Previously, she curated the 2015 edition of *Operae*, the independent design festival based in Turin (Italy), and the exhibition and catalogue *Ugo la Pietra. Disequilibrating Design* (2014) for the Triennale Design Museum in Milan. She has been design editor for Abitare magazine (2011-2013) and curated the editorial project of Icon Design magazine (2015-

2017). Until 2016 she taught at the School of Design of the Politecnico di Milano and at the Master of Interior Design program at the Nuova Accademia di Belle Arti in Milan. She currently teaches at the Social Design Master of the Design Academy Eindhoven.

List of References

Agamben G., 2005, *State of Exception*, The University of Chicago Press, Chicago

Akoaki, 2017, *Discovering Detroit*, International Design Biennale, St. Etienne, retrieved on 4 August 2018 at http://www.biennale-design.com/saint-etienne/2017/en/detroit/

Anderson S., 2016, *Insecurities: Tracing Displacement and Shelter*, MoMA, New York, retrieved on 4 April 2017 at https://www.moma.org/calendar/exhibitions/1653

Anzaldúa G., 1987, *Borderlands/la frontera. The new mestiza*, Aunt Lute Books, San Francisco

Augé, M. 2005, *An interview with Marc Augé: "Tourism could well be the last utopia"*

Berardi F. "Bifo", 2009, *The Soul at Work. From Alienation to Autonomy*, The MIT Press, Semiotext(e), Cambridge, Massachusetts

Berger J., 2016, *Confabulations*, pp. 139-140, Penguin Books UK, London

Bergmann F., 2014, *New Work Life: New Business Enterprises Ten Years and Now!*, CreateSpace Independent Publishing Platform, Scotts Valley

Bey H., 1994, *Immediatism*, AK Press, Cico

Bodei R., 2016, *Borders/Il limite*, Il Mulino, Bologna

Bourdieu P., 1998, *Acts of Resistance. Against the New Myths of our Time*, p. 7, Polity Press, Cambridge

Boym S., 2007, *Nostalgia and its Discontents*, The Hedgehog Review, 9:2 Summer 2007

Braidotti R., 2013, *The Post-human: Life Beyond the Individual, Species, Death*, Polity Press, Cambridge

Bratton B., 2013, *Some Trace Effects of the Post-Anthropocene: On Accelerationist Geopolitical Aesthetics*, e-flux journal, 46, pp1-12

Bridle J., 2015, *Citizen Ex*, retrieved on 3 January 2016 at http://jamesbridle.com/works/citizen-ex

Brown W., 2005, *Edgework, Critical Essays on Knowledge and Politics*, cap. IV, Princeton University Press, Princeton

Chozick A., 2010, *Motown Becomes Movietown*, The Wall Street Journal, retrieved on 14 August 2018 at https://www.wsj.com/articles/SB10001424052748703743504575493773596572154

Colomina B. and Wigley M., 2016, in *Design Has Gone Viral, but Design Community Is Stranded*, interview by Amy Frearson, Dezeen, retrieved on 21 September 2016 at https://www.dezeen.com/2016/09/21/mark-wigley-beatriz-colomina-istanbul-design-biennial-curators-interview/

Colomina B. and Wigley M., 2016, *Superhumanity at the 3rd Istanbul Design Biennial*, e-flux, retrieved on 29 March 2019 at http://www.e-flux.com/announcements/63447/superhumanity-at-the-3rd-istanbul-design-biennial/

Crutzen P., 2005, *Welcome to the Anthropocene. Man Has Changed the Climate, the Earth Enters a New Era*, Mondadori, Milano

DAAR, 2007, *Decolonizing Architecture Art Residency* in http://www.decolo nizing.ps/site/

Davis M., 2006, *Planet of Slums*, Verso, New York

Deleuze G. and Guattari F., 1983, *The Anti-Oedipus: Capitalism and Schizophrenia*, University of Minnesota Press, Minneapolis

DeLillo D., 2017, *Zero K*, Scribner, New York

Franzen J., 2010, *Freedom*, Farrar, Straus and Giroux, New York

Griziotti G., 2016, *Neurocapitalism. Technological Mediations and Lines of Escape*, p. 120, Mimesis, Sesto San Giovanni

Groys B., 2009, *Art Power*, MIT Press, Cambridge, Massachusetts

Gundle S., 2009, *Glamour: A History*, Oxford University Press, Oxford

Harvey D. cited in Carlson S., 2014, *Mapping a New Economy*, The Chronicle of Higher Education, retrieved on 27 May 2014 at http://chronicle.com/article/Mapping-a-New-Economy/146433/

Helliwell, J., Layard, R., Sachs, J., 2012, *World Happiness Report 2012*, Sustainable Development Solutions Network, New York

Houellebecq M., 2015, *Submission*, Groupe Flammarion, Paris

Hyperakt and Ijeoma E., 2014, *The Refugee Project*, MoMA, New York, retrieved on 4 April 2017 at http://www.therefugeeproject.org/

Katz B., 2015, *Make It New. A History of Silicon Valley Design*, MIT Press, Cambridge, Massachusetts

Laboria Cuboniks, 2014, *The Xenofeminist Manifesto* in http://www.laboria cuboniks.net/index.html

Land N., 2018, *Fanged Noumena: Collected Writings 1987–2007*, MIT Press, Cambridge, Massachusetts

Latour B., 1991, *Nous N'avons Jamais Été Modernes: Essais D'anthropologie Symétrique*, La Découverte, Paris

Latour B. and Leclerq C., 2016, *Reset Modernity*, co-published with ZKM | Center for Art and Media, Karlsruhe, MIT Press, Cambridge, Massachusetts

Lepore J. cited in Goldstein E., 2018, *The Academy Is Largely Itself Responsible for Its Own Peril*, The Chronicle Review, retrieved on 13 November 2018 at https://www.chronicle.com/article/The-Academy-Is-Largely/245080?cid= wsinglestory_41_1

Lomas R., 1999, *The Man Who Invented the Twentieth Century*, Headline, London

Mari E., 2014, *Sono Comunista, Interview with Francesca Esposito*, Klat Magazine, retrieved on 14 January 2019 at http://www.klatmagazine.com/design/enzo-mari-sono-comunista-interview/11567

Masco, J., 2010, *Bad Weather: On Planetary Crisis*, Social Studies of Science 40:1 pp. 7-40, Sage Journals, New York

Mason P., 2015, *Postcapitalism. A Guide to Our Future*, Penguin Books UK, London

Mason P., 2016, *I Consigli Del Postcapitalista Paul Mason*, Internazionale, retrieved on 14 January 2019 at https://www.internazionale.it/festival/notizie/2016/09/16/paul-mason-ferrara-festival

May D. cited in Shuja H., 2017, *Letter of Recommendation: Detroit Techno*, The New York Times Magazine, retrieved on 10 June 2018 at https://www.nytimes.com/2017/07/13/magazine/letter-of-recommendation-detroit-techno.html

May D., 2013, *Derrick May: 'I Stick Around in Detroit Because It's My Home No 1'*, interview by Reidy T., The Guardian, retrieved on 15 January 2019 at https://www.theguardian.com/music/2013/nov/20/derrick-may-techno-detroit-home

McGuirk J., 2011, *Korea's Design Biennial: An Extreme Body of Work That Pushes No Products*, The Guardian, retrieved on 12 January 2019 at https://www.theguardian.com/artanddesign/2011/sep/06/korea-design-biennial-gwangju

Midgley M., 1979, *Brutality and Sentimentality, Philosophy*, Volume 54, Issue 209, pp. 385-389, Philosophy Journal, Cambridge University Press, Cambridge

Morton, T., 2013, *Hyperorbjects: Philosophy and Ecology after the End of the World*, Minnesota University Press, Minneapolis

Muzi M., Petroni M., 2017, *Refusal Party*, BIO25, retrieved 14 January 2019 at on https://bio.si/en/program/events/9/2017-05-26/22-00/refusal-party/

Nordt C., et al., 2015, *Modelling suicide and unemployment: a longitudinal analysis covering 63 countries, 2000–11*, 2(3):239-45, Lancet Psychiatry, Elsevier, Amsterdam

Papanek, V.J., 1984, *Design for the Real World: Human Ecology and Social Change*, Van Nostrand Reinhold Co., New York

Papapetros S., 2012, *On the Animation of the Inorganic: Art, Architecture, and the Extension of Life*, University of Chicago Press, Chicago

Parasite2.0, 2017, *Cartha – On Making Heimat,* Park Books, Chicago

Pasquinelli M., 2014, *The Algorithms of Capital. Accelerationism, Machines of Knowledge, and Municipal Autonomy*, Ombrecorte, Verona

Petroni M, 2017, *Zero Degree Design,* Domus Web, retrieved on 10 January 2019 at https://www.domusweb.it/en/interviews/2017/02/24/akoaki_zero_degree_design.html

Petroni M., 2016, *Worlds Within Reach/Mondi Possibili, Appunti di Teoria del Design*, Edizioni Temporale, Milan

Petroni M., 2016, *Silence in Beirut*, Domus Web, retrieved on 12 January 2019 at http://www.domusweb.it/it/design/2016/09/22/silence_beirut.html

Polanyi K., 1944, *The Great Transformation: The origins of our time*, Farrar & Rinehart, New York

Ranciere J., 2000, *Le Partage Du Sensible: Esthétique Et Politique*, La Fabrique editions, Paris

Renn M.A., 2009, *Detroit: Urban Laboratory and the New American Frontier*, New Geography, retrieved on 3 November 2018 at http://www.newgeography.com/content/001171-detroit-urban-laboratory-and-new-american-frontier

Rockström, J., et al., 2009, *A Safe Operating Space for Humanity*, Nature, vol. 461, pp. 472-475, London

Rozendaal R., 2015, *Haiku 154*, Rozendaal Website, retrieved on 2 January 2019 at https://www.newrafael.com/rr-haiku-154/

Rushkoff D., 2013, *Present Shock: When Everything Happens Now*, p. 252, Penguin Random House, New York

Said E., 1993, *Culture and Imperialism*, Chatto and Windus, London

Salzani C., 2012, *Giorgio Agamben's Anti-Utopia*, Utopian Studies, Vol. 23, Number 1, p. 212, Penn State University Press, University Park, Pennsylvania

Sassen S., 2015, *Espulsioni. Brutalità E Complessità Nell'economia Globale (Expulsions. Brutality and Complexity in The Global Econony)*, p. 37, Il Mulino, Bologna

Scarpa T., 2016, *Il Brevetto del Geco*, Einaudi, Torino

Snyder R. 2013, *Governor Rick Snyder Authorizes Detroit Bankruptcy Filing (Youtube Video)*, retrieved on 2 January 2019 at https://www.youtube.com/watch?v=h0WKENzYcTU

Sottsass E. Jr. and Bill M., 1983, *Design and Theory: Two Points of View", in Design Since 1945*, edited by Hiesinger K.B. and Marcus G.H., p. 3., Rizzoli, New York

Srnicek N and Williams A., 2016, *Inventing the Future: Postcapitalism and A World Without Work*, p. 47, Verso Books, New York

Steyerl H. et al., 2019, *The Wretched of the Screen*, Sternberg Press/e-flux journal, Berlin

Tafuri M., in Assennato M., 2016, *La domanda irrisolta di Manfredo Tafuri*, Operaviva Magazine, retrieved on 3 June 2018 at http://operaviva.info/la-domanda-irrisolta-di-manfredo-tafuri/

Thwaites T., 2011, *The Toaster Project or A Heroic Attempt to Build A Simple Electric Appliance from Scratch*, Princeton Architectural Press, New York

Tiravanija R., 2016, *Do Not Ever Work*, OneStar Press, Paris

Toffler A., 1970, *Future Shock*, Random House, New York

van Tuinen, S., 2009, *Air Conditioning Spaceship Earth: Peter Sloterdijk's Ethico-Aesthetic Paradigm*, Environment and Planning D: Society and Space, 27, pp. 105-118, Sage Journals, New York

Zizek S., 2010, *Living in the End Times*, Verso Books, New York

Index

vampire, 1
Ventimiglia, 24, 25
Victor Papanek, vi, 35
violence, 23, 25, 32

W

Wall Street Journal, 4

Walmart, 38
Wendy Brown, 32
worker, 43

Z

Zeno Franchini, 25
zombie, 1

www.ingramcontent.com/pod-product-compliance
Lightning Source LLC
Chambersburg PA
CBHW071058280326
41928CB00050B/2548